JAPANESE
ARMY
HANDBOOK
1939-1945

Tankettes on a victory parade. / *IWM*

JAPANESE ARMY HANDBOOK 1939-1945

A.J.Barker

HIPPOCRENE
BOOKS, INC.

Acknowledgements and Bibliography

The assistance of Mr K. M. White, Librarian at the Staff College, Camberley, is gratefully acknowledged.

Because of the language problem there is a dearth of material on the technical aspects of Japanese armament, and apart from the Penguin Special *How the Jap Army Fights* (published by Penguin Books and the *US Infantry Journal* in June 1942), most of the available information has been extracted from wartime classified publications not generally available to the public.

For the illustrations I must thank the Director and Photographic Librarian of the Imperial War Museum, and the publishers of Imperial Japanese Army and Navy Uniforms and Equipment.

First published 1979 in the United States
by Hippocrene Books Inc,
171 Madison Avenue,
New York NY 10016

Printed in Great Britain
Library of Congress Catalog Card Number 79-84381
ISBN 0-88254-484-5

All colour artwork provided by
Bryan Fosten

 Contents

Japanese soldiers loading a medium
tank M2594. / *IWM*

Chapter 1
The Japanese Soldier

The source of strength for any military power lies in its people, from whom the common soldier is drawn. In 1939 there were approximately 100 million Japanese citizens, 70 million of them in Japan proper. Japan was a hardworking nation, eking out its sustenance from the often barren land of those myriads of tight islands, and it retained its competitiveness in commerce through the willingness of its workers to work longer hours for less pay. The standard of living was low but the level of literacy fairly high. It had an economy and a psychology which produced soldiers who were strong and willing, who were accustomed to hardships perhaps greater than those in the normal course of military life, and who accepted military service as an inevitable and honourable thing.

In World War II the Japanese soldier proved a tough enemy — daring in attack, stubborn in defence. Even when his position seemed hopeless to him he usually fought on to the death. Right up to the end of the war he showed little readiness to surrender and almost always preferred to die in battle or take his own life rather than fall into the hands of his enemies. Few Japanese prisoners surrendered voluntarily; most of them were either too weak or too ill to offer any resistance or to commit suicide.

The reasons for the Japanese soldier's attitude and stern discipline lay in his early upbringing, his education, and his Army training. For several centuries before Japan adopted a European army system and introduced conscription (1872), the old warrior class — the Samurai — was held in high esteem. The makers of the twentieth century Japanese Army were quick to realise the advantages to be gained by continuing to foster this spirit, and so, by every means possible, the heroism and noble calling of the warrior were praised. When Japan started on warlike ventures and came out victorious, the prestige of the Army grew. The Japanese Army thus came to occupy a unique position in Japan and for the 10 years before World War II it played a major part in governing the nation.

Conscripts constituted the bulk of the army, and in normal times the term of service was two years. Most of the men in the ranks were peasants well suited to army life since their harsh frugal existence on Japanese farms had inured them to hardships. They were stocky, well built with powerful backs accustomed to carrying heavy burdens, and — at the same time — simple, docile and obedient.

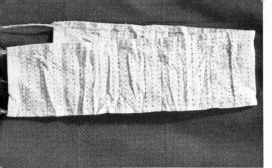
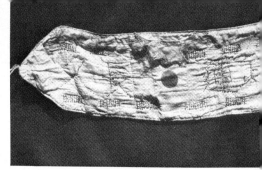
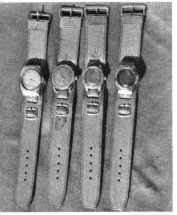

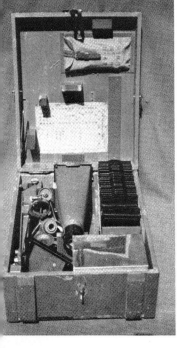
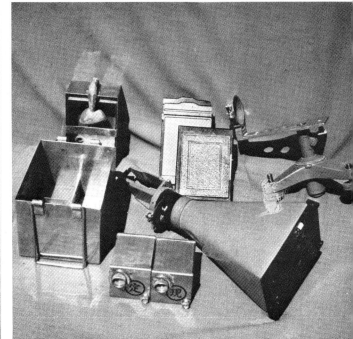

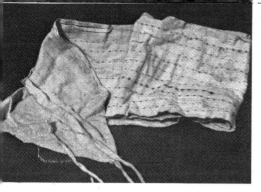
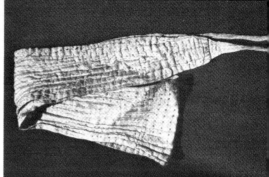

Above and right: Senninbari (1,000 stitches belt). These cloth body belts, fabricated by wives and sweethearts were supposed to bring luck to the Japanese soldiers who wore them.

Centre left: Japanese issue watches.

Bottom left: Type 96 range-finder camera and container.

Below: Bullet-proof vests. These were not a general issue and were probably only used by senior officers and diplomats.

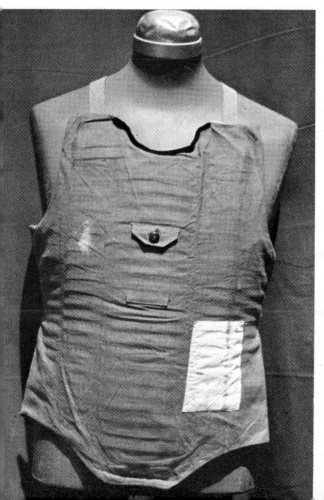

Any male between the ages of 20 and 40 was eligible for military service and with an intake of about 150,000 conscripts a year the Japanese had a standing army of about 375,000 at the time of Pearl Harbor and about two million trained reserves. After the mobilisation which preceded Pearl Harbor the call-up age was lowered from 20 to 19 and the military service age raised from 40 to 45. Peacetime training programmes were also cut and by 1942 infantry soldiers were receiving as little as three months training before being sent to operational areas. (In many instances some training was given in operational areas — China being used as a theatre where troops could gain combat experience). The training periods of technical troops, such as signals and engineer personnel, were also reduced.

NCOs and officers were mostly recruited from young men who had attended higher educational establishments. Most of the regular officers were graduates of the Military Academy while NCOs were trained at one or other of the NCO schools in Japan and Manchuria.

Training at all levels was generally intense and thorough, and before he was sent to an operational area a Japanese soldier was instructed not only how to use his weapons but the reasons why he should fight and why he should not be beaten. He must live according to the Japanese soldiers 'code' — a directive covering three pages of very involved logic in very fine print which consisted, in brief, of five points:

1 The soldier should consider loyalty his essential duty. 'Remember that the protection of the state and the maintenance of its power depend upon the strength of its arms ... Bear in mind that duty is weightier than a mountain, while death is lighter than a feather.'
2 The soldier should be strict in observing propriety. 'Inferiors should regard the orders of their superiors as issuing directly from Us' (the emperor).
3 The soldier should esteem valour. 'Never to despise an inferior enemy, or to fear a superior, but to do one's duty as a soldier or sailor — that is true valour.'
4 The soldier should highly value faithfulness and righteousness. 'Faithfulness implies the keeping of one's word, and righteousness the fulfilment of one's duty.'
5 The soldier should make simplicity his aim. 'If you do not make simplicity your aim, you will become effeminate or frivolous and acquire fondness for luxurious and extravagant ways.'

Finally, in the event of being prisoner, a Japanese soldier knew that he would be dishonoured and his family would have no pension. If on the other hand he died fighting he was assured of reward — his family would be honoured and receive a pension, and if possible his ashes would be sent back to Japan and buried at the national shrine of Yasekuni.

As a result of this system and training the Japanese soldier was highly disciplined, brave and ready to fight to the bitter end rather than surrender. And this attitude persisted even when he became conscious of Allied superiority in weapons and equipment.

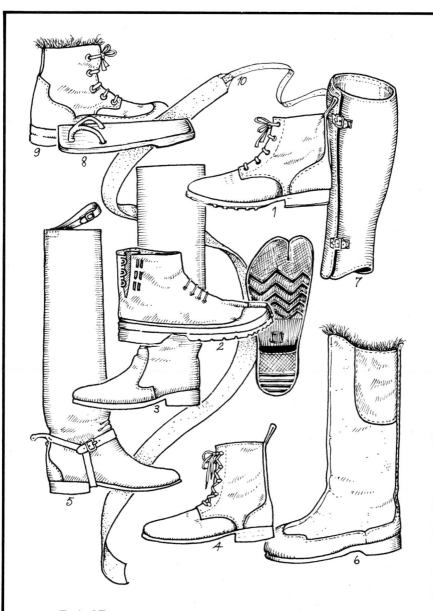

Typical Footwear:

1 Other rank's brown marching boot.
2 The 'Tabi'.
3 Officer's high boot.
4 Officer's black marching boot.
5 Officer's riding boot.
6 Fur lined high felt boot.
7 Leather gaiter used by officers.
8 Fatigue footwear.
9 Fur lined boot.
10 Puttee or leg wrapping. / *Bryan Fosten*

On active service a Japanese private soldier was paid 10 yen (about £1 or $2) a month. Eight yen went home to his family, 1%₁₀ yen was deducted for compulsory savings, and the rest was his to squander or keep.

Personal equipment was simple but practical. With a full complement of ammunition and rations the Japanese infantryman carried a load of about five kilograms. His helmet, which weighed another kilogram, had a high crown for protection against shrapnel and was an inconspicuous tan in colour — as was the star insignia on the helmet. In North China the helmet was often worn bonnet-fashion with straps tied under the chin and with a padded cloth as an inner liner to keep out the biting cold. A coarse net to hold leaves and twigs as camouflage was commonly worn over the helmet in the field.

For all ranks the army uniform was khaki in colour. (Marines and sailors dressed in the conventional blue and white). In North China and Manchuria great-coats of Australian wool were issued for wear in cold weather, together with a fur lining to go inside the soft cap which was the normal headgear. Footwear consisted of black or brown hobnailed boots, or — in hot climates — 'tobi' (canvas shoes with heavy rubber soles in which the big toe was separated from the remainder of the foot) were worn. Khaki woollen puttees were invariably worn by other ranks, and sometimes by junior officers. Belts and ammunition pouches were of heavy well-tanned leather.

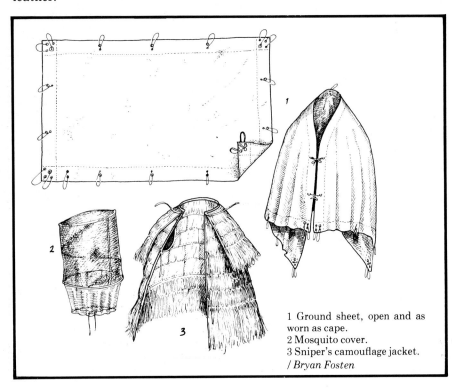

1 Ground sheet, open and as worn as cape.
2 Mosquito cover.
3 Sniper's camouflage jacket.
/ Bryan Fosten

12

Chapter 2

Organisation of the Japanese Army

Before turning to Japanese armament a brief review of the organisation of Japanese units is desirable.

First, it must be understood that the Japanese Army of World War II was not a rigid organisation. Until 1936 its basic formation was a ponderous square-type (four-brigade/regiment) infantry division, some 25,000 strong. These divisions proved to be inflexible, and weak in transport, artillery and automatic weapons. After 1936, however, the enterprises on which the masters of Japan embarked involved the army in a wide range of military tasks in the most diverse conditions — mopping up guerillas in the interior of China, guarding extended lines of communications, garrisoning the empty spaces of the Manchurian and Mongolian borders. seizing and endeavouring to hold the long coast lines and countless islands of the East Indies and the South Seas. So, to meet these and other demands the Japanese War Office was compelled to adopt more flexible organisations and to create special forces to discharge the Army's tasks in order to make the most economical use of the men and material available.

The infantry division remained the basic Army formation, but the old four brigade formation was replaced by a triangular division. This formation, which by 1939 had become standard formation and was known as the B type (*Otsu*) division, consisted of three infantry regiments, a field (or mountain) artillery regiment, an engineer regiment, a reconnaissance unit, a transport regiment, and the usual service troops.*

Standard infantry divisions with additional artillery under command and bigger infantry battalions with extra weapons which existed in Manchuria and North China were probably relics of the original square type formations. Known as A type (*Ko*) divisions, they were not intended for jungle warfare and some of them had a tank battalion as well as the reconnaissance unit.

The third type of division was the 'Garrison' or C type (*Hei*) — a weaker formation organised into two brigades each of four infantry battalions with fewer weapons than the battalions of a standard division. As their name implies, such divisions were employed mainly on garrison duties and their

---

* The organisation of the standard (B type), strengthened
(A type) and 'Garrison' (C type) Japanese division is illustrated in Appendix 1.

brigade organisation was designed to allow them to be split up and used independently in anti-guerilla operations.

In addition to the three different types of division the Japanese picture is complicated by the existence of many independent brigades organised and equipped for special roles or for employment in particular theatres. Independent mixed brigades were employed in China for example — mainly on garrison or anti-guerilla duties. Such brigades were predominantly a rifle force composed usually of between three and six infantry battalions 750 to 900 strong, together with relatively small artillery, engineer, and signals units. Battalions had three or four rifle companies and their strength varied accordingly. Other independent mixed brigades and regiments operated in South-East Asia, the Netherlands East Indies and in the Central Pacific. Because the brigade organisation suited to China did not contain enough of the heavier infantry weapons to operate against more powerfully equipped armies than the Chinese the new brigades were given heavier fire power in the infantry battalions — in particular mortars and anti-tank guns were introduced. Brigades of this type had from four to eight infantry battalions, an artillery unit of three companies, an engineer unit and a signals unit and brigade headquarters varied in strength according to the number of attached specialists. In addition, some brigades had an anti-aircraft company and some had a tank unit. At full strength these brigades varied from 3,100 to about 6,000 according to their composition.

The brigade commander was a major-general — usually a man who had been an infantry group commander in a standard infantry division.*

To defend islands in the Pacific independent mixed regiments were extensively used. Such regiments consisted of forces of infantry and supporting arms — similar to but smaller than the independent brigades. Such regiments normally comprised two or three independent infantry battalions and supporting artillery, engineer and signals units. They could also have a small tank unit or a company of anti-aircraft artillery, and some regiments did not have an engineer unit.

Apart from the divisional and brigade group formations other infantry organisations also existed in 1939 or were created during the next five years. For example the 'Fortress' coast artillery — found in Japan proper, Korea, Formosa, the Bonin Islands, the Ryukyu Islands and Manchuria — contained an infantry element whose role it was to defend the fixed coastal artillery installations. Every fortress command was organised according to its own particular circumstances. The nucleus in each case was a coast defence heavy artillery unit, supplemented sometimes by a field or mountain artillery unit and anything from one to four fortress infantry units.

Cavalry
Cavalry regiments took the place of the reconnaissance or tank units in some of the infantry divisions. Additionally the Japanese maintained a few

* The organisation of a typical mixed brigade is shown in Appendix 2.

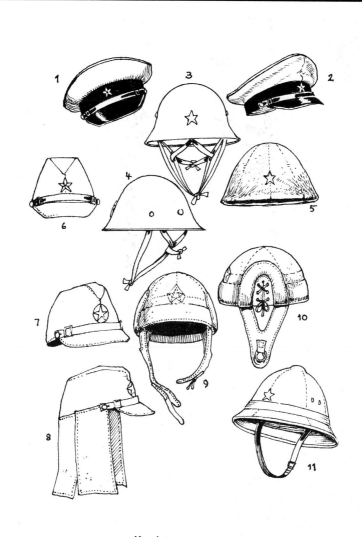

Headgear.
1 Officer's cap.
2 Other rank's cap.
3/4 Standard issue helmet.
5 Helmet with cover.
6 Officer's field cap.
7 Other rank's field cap
8 Field cap with neck cover.
9/10 Paratroop's helmet.
11 Tropical helmet.

Above left: Winter wear for tank crews.

Above centre: Summer wear for tank crews.

Above right: Artillery sergeant-major.

Below: From left to right: 1930 Officer's tunic; 1930 Other rank's tunic; 1938 Officer's tunic; 1938 Other rank's tunic. / *Bryan Fosten*

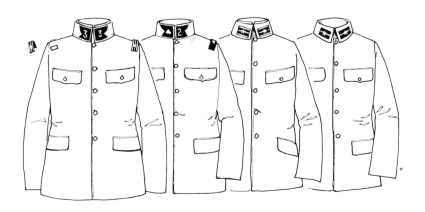

independent cavalry brigades. They consisted of two regiments — of four rifle and sabre companies and one machine gun company — and supporting arms. (Of the latter the most important was the horse artillery regiment of two companies each with four medium mortars or 75mm field guns). The rifle and sabre companies, each with a nominal strength of 140 all ranks, had three rifle platoons and a machine gun platoon; and the machine gun company included an anti-tank platoon with two 37mm guns.

Armour

During the Sino-Japanese war Japanese tankettes and light tanks were used against the Chinese, and medium tanks were employed in Malaya in 1942. But there was no call for panzer-type formations until a defeat by Russian armour at Nomonhan caused the Japanese General Staff to revise their ideas of deploying tanks only in penny packets. Armoured divisions did not come into being immediately but some tank regiments (*Sensha Rentai*) were brigaded into groups. These tank groups (*Sensha Dan*) consisted simply of three or four tank regiments, together with supply and maintenance services; there was no infantry or other supporting arms which would have enabled them to operate in an independent role. With infantry the tanks groups became the tank brigades (*Sensha Ryodan*) one of which became the nucleus of an armoured division (*Sensha Shidan*) formed in 1943 for service in Manchuria.

The composition of the tank regiment varied, but the average strength was 850 officers and men, with 80 tanks — of which two or three were first line replacement vehicles.† Independent tank companies consisting of 12 tanks under command of a captain operated in the South-West Pacific, but these were companies detached from regular tank regiments. However, a number of independent tankette companies, equipped with 17 tankettes and 16 armoured trailers were raised — primarily for use as supply vehicles in forward areas in the Pacific theatre.

Artillery

Artillery was not classified by the Japanese in exactly the same way as in the British and American armies. The lighter guns were 'field' and 'mountain', and everything heavier than a 105mm (4.14in) howitzer was 'heavy'. In effect what the Japanese called 'heavy artillery' could really be divided broadly into three categories, 'field heavy' and 'heavy' which had some degree of mobility, and 'fortress' which was fixed coast-defence artillery. Japanese terms and the equivalents were as follows:

Yahohei	Field artillery
Sampohei	Mountain artillery
Yasen Juhohei	Medium artillery (literally 'Field heavy artillery')
Yuhoei	Heavy artillery
Yosai Juhohei	Fortress artillery
Regiment (*Rentai*)	Regiment

† See Appendix 3 for the organisation of a tank regiment.

Battalion (*Daitai*)	Battery
Company (*Chutai*)	Troop
Platoon (*Shotai*)	Section
Section (*Buntai*)	Sub-section

Field Artillery

Standard Japanese divisions contained a field artillery regiment of a headquarters and three artillery battalions. Each battalion had three companies of a headquarters and two gun platoons with the latter sub-divided into two sections of one 75mm gun apiece. The complete regiment could thus deploy 36 guns, and its total strength was about 2,300 men. Type A divisions included an artillery group headquarters under a colonel or major-general, who functioned as a British CRA and commanded the field, mountain and anti-aircraft batteries attached to the division as well as the regular artillery regiment. The organisation of the latter was different in so far as it had four battalions each of three companies — with three of the battalions being equipped with eight 105mm howitzers and four 75mm guns while the remaining battalion had 12 105mm howitzers. On paper 'garrison' divisions had no artillery units but some of them were allotted artillery regiments on a reduced establishment consisting of three battalions each of eight 75mm guns and with an approximate strength of 1,500 men.

Independent artillery battalions, like battalions of divisional field artillery, consisted of three companies each of four guns, with company and battalion transport — twelve 75mm guns in all. The strength of a battalion of divisional field artillery, horse-drawn, was about 680 officers and men and an independent battalion of horse-drawn artillery needed more men to operate independently. (In practice this gave it an establishment of about 750).

Mountain Artillery

Mountain artillery carried on pack horses or mules — with each gun constituting six to eight animal loads — was the normal Japanese artillery in South-East Asia and the South-West Pacific. Mountain artillery regiments were organised similarly to the field artillery regiments which they often replaced. Each regiment had three battalions, each of three companies with four 75mm mountain guns apiece. However some field artillery regiments which were converted into mountain artillery regiments for service in jungle country were in fact given only 27 (instead of 36) mountain guns, and independent mountain artillery regiments operated with only two battalions and consequently had only 24 guns.

Medium Artillery

Apart from the 'Field Heavy artillery' battalion equipped with 150mm howitzers found in the Type A divisional artillery, the bulk of the Japanese medium artillery was organised into independent units and allotted to armies on an as required basis. The principal Japanese medium artillery weapons were the tractor-drawn 105mm gun and the 150mm howitzer in two types — the old horse-drawn 1915 model and the Type 96 (1936)

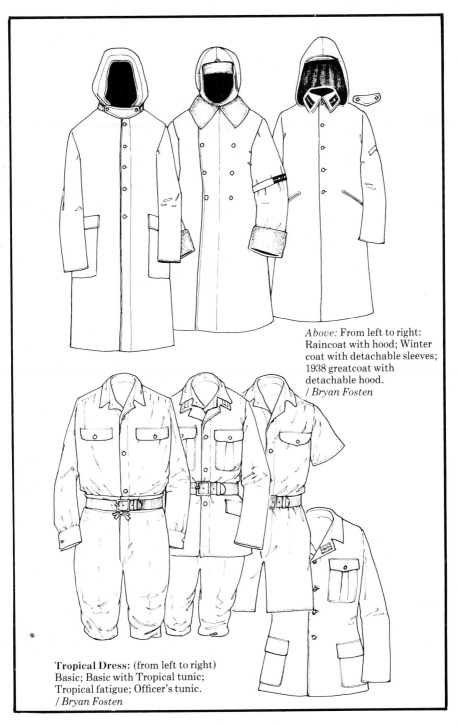

Above: From left to right: Raincoat with hood; Winter coat with detachable sleeves; 1938 greatcoat with detachable hood. / *Bryan Fosten*

Tropical Dress: (from left to right) Basic; Basic with Tropical tunic; Tropical fatigue; Officer's tunic. / *Bryan Fosten*

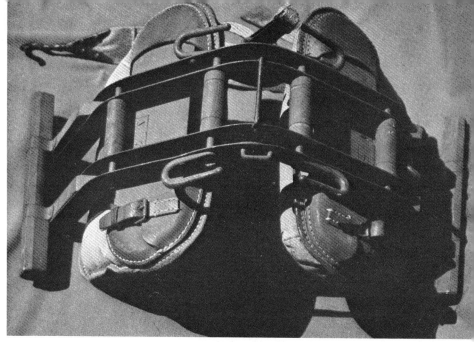

Above: Pack-animal saddle for artillery loads.

Centre right: Hand-driven generator.

Bottom right: Anti-gas first-aid kit.

号 二
箱急救スガ

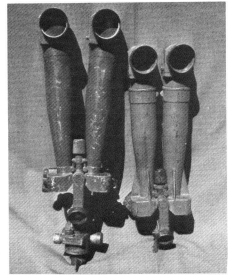

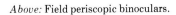

Above: Field periscopic binoculars.

Left: Japanese issue binoculars.

Bottom left: Type 96 clinometer for Type 92 HMG.

Below: Compass/clinometer on tripod.

tractor-drawn model. There was also a longer-range weapon, the Type 18 (1929) 150mm gun, tractor-drawn.

According to which of these weapons were carried the organisation varied. A medium gun howitzer regiment, for example, equipped with 150mm howitzers with either motor or animal transport, had two battalions each of three companies, and companies consisted of two platoons of two gun sections with one 150mm howitzer apiece, ie a total of 24 150mm howitzers. On the other hand, while a medium gun regiment also contained two battalions, these had only two companies each (of two platoons). Thus the total number of 105mm guns in such a regiment was only 16.

Heavy Artillery and Miscellaneous Field Artillery units

There was no fixed establishment for 'heavy artillery' proper in the Japanese army but 24cm (9.4in) howitzers and larger calibre weapons existed although they were rarely used in the field.

By Western standards Japanese counter-battery organisations were neither strong nor effective. And few artillery intelligence regiments actually existed. Nevertheless there were occasions, as at Hong Kong for example, where Japanese produced effective counter-battery fire. Observation balloons were employed by the Japanese artillery in the assault on Singapore but this was the only occasion that a Japanese observation balloon unit is known to have been deployed.

Anti-Aircraft Artillery

The bulk of Japanese anti-aircraft artillery was made up of independent units assigned as required. Anti-aircraft protection was not their only task, since the Japanese relied on their anti-aircraft gunners for anti-tank fire-power also.

A Japanese AA regiment employed in a static role consisted of two AA gun battalions and a searchlight battalion, with a total of 48 75mm AA guns and 24 searchlights. While the static battalion had 24 guns, a mobile battalion had only 12 75mm guns supplemented by six AA machine guns.

A field 'machine cannon' company also existed. Armed with six 20mm dual purpose AA and anti-tank machine guns these companies could be transported either in motor vehicles or by pack animals. Searchlight battalions had two companies, each of two platoons of three sections with a searchlight and sound locator in each section.

Anti-tank Artillery

Unlike its anti-aircraft artillery the majority of anti-tank units in the Japanese Army were integrated in the infantry divisions. A few independent anti-tank battalions did exist however. These were normally 12-gun units, equipped either with 37mm weapons or the more modern 47mm anti-tank guns. Such battalions were either motorised (ie with tractor-drawn guns), horse-drawn or pack. Organised into a battalion headquarters, three anti-tank companies — each of two platoons of two sections of one gun apiece — and a battalion ammunition train the nominal strength was 458 all ranks. Unlike the companies in an anti-tank battalion

Telecommunication equipment.

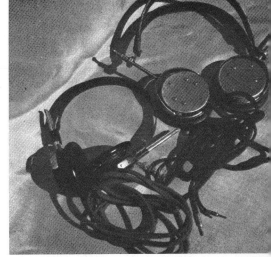

an independent anti-tank company was an eight gun unit of four platoons. Like the battalion it could have either motor, horse or pack transport, and its strength varied accordingly.

Mortar Units
Until late 1943 Japanese mortar units were almost all army troops, but after 1943 such units were parcelled out to lower formations. By 1945 the 'artillery' of some of the mixed brigades was a mortar unit. Amphibious brigades were also equipped with mortars and in some infantry battalions mortars replaced the standard 70mm close-support howitzer in the battalion gun platoon. But independent mortar units continued to exist until the end of the war. Those officered and manned by gunners were known as *Kyuho* units, while those which were infantry units were termed *Hakugeki*.†

The standard mortar battalion (*Hakugeki Daitai*) was equipped with 36 81mm mortars. It had a headquarters which contained observers, signalmen and transport; a battalion ammunition train; and three mortar companies with 12 mortars each, and it could have horse transport or be motorised. Medium mortar battalions (*Chu Hakugeki Daitai*) which had a similar organisation but carried only 12 medium 15cm artillery mortars, were mainly horse-drawn units.

Finally there were the independent artillery mortar battalions (*Dokuritsu Kyuho Daitai*), equipped with Type 98 250mm spigot mortars which were used to considerable effect in Burma. These mortars, eight of which formed the armament of the battalion, were ponderous short-range weapons but they could hurl a 700lb bomb. (Because of the short life of the weapon each battalion was issued with eight spare mortars as first-line replacements).

Engineers
The Japanese engineer arm in World War II consisted of divisional engineers and a variety of independent units which are discussed in Chapter 6. Japanese divisional commanders generally appear to have treated their own engineers more as an expendable commodity than British, American or German divisional commanders; in addition to their strictly engineer duties — fieldwork, demolitions, mine-clearing, river crossing and so on — they were often called upon to provide assault detachments for tasks which would clearly be costly and even suicidal.

Organisation of the divisional engineer regiment was four companies — three field companies and a stores company — with a total establishment of 900-1,000 men. This organisation was designed to allow sub-allotment of a field company to each of the three infantry regiments in the standard division. (In 'garrison' divisions there was usually only a small engineer unit consisting of an HQ and three platoons). Each field company carried shovels, pick-axes, felling axes, wire-cutters, hand axes, bill hooks, saws etc besides a small amount of tradesmen's tools and technical instruments. Bridging

---

† To confuse matters, some artillery mortar units were also called *Hakugeki* if they were armed with medium (15cm) or lighter mortars.

Japanese radio and signal equipment.

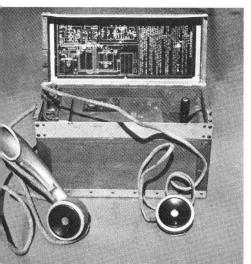

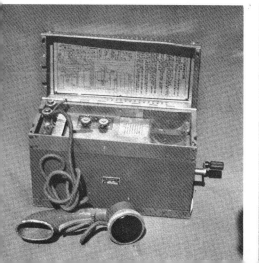

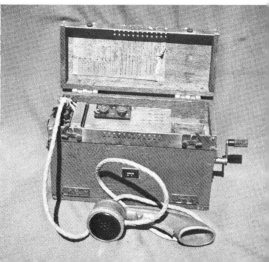

equipment in the division was generally limited to assault boats, rubber boats, and sometimes assault bridges and pontoons. Engineers were equipped with short rifles (Meiji 38s), LMGs, and occasionally with flame throwers.

Signals

One feature of Japanese signals' organisations was the emphasis on simplicity and flexibility. Each division had a divisional signals unit consisting of four platoons (two line platoons, one wireless and one stores platoon) with a total establishment of 250 officers and men. Standard equipment comprised 30 miles of wire, 32 telephones and 8-10 radio sets. Communication above division was controlled by signals regiments organised according to need, and made up of a number of small independent signals units. Army headquarters had their own signals section and possibly a carrier pigeon section, together with a signals unit to coordinate the signals networks of anti-aircraft organisations, specialist radio units to operate fixed radio stations and possibly special radio units to operate direct on finding equipment.

Miscellaneous Specialist Troops

Japanese special forces are discussed in Chapters 6 and 7. But various specialist troops which were formed in the divisional organisations deserve a brief mention. Water purification units were counted as part of the medical division of the infantry division. With a strength of about 50 men, all of whom were medical orderlies, such units were responsible for the water supply of the division.

Veterinary units of four officers and 46 men were attached to units with horse and pack transport. Such units contained treatment, supply and farrier sections to deal with casualties to animals in the division.

Finally some divisions included chemical warfare units. Selected men were trained as 'gas personnel' in all infantry divisions, and some of them were formed into smoke companies with apparatus capable of being employed in chemical warfare. The chemical warfare units, on the other hand, were solely designed for decontamination and gas control duties. With a total establishment of 150-250 men, they were organised into three field platoons of three sections and a supply column of three sections.

In fact, the Japanese did not attempt to use gas as a weapon although there were reports that it was used in China on several occasions. (In October 1937 the use of gas by the Japanese Army — probably mustard — was the subject of a protest of the League of Nations, and in September 1938 the Chinese claimed two of their regiments were wiped out by gas in an engagement in the Yangtze valley near Juichang). Japanese infantry in pre-World War II manoeuvres carried gas masks in heavy wooden boxes, but during the war these were discarded. (The little filters worn by fastidious Japanese to keep the dust and airborne germs out of their nostrils, were sometimes worn by Japanese soldiers and civilians in China, and these were undoubtedly frequently mistaken for gas masks).

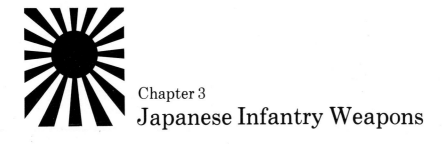

Chapter 3
Japanese Infantry Weapons

European arms were first introduced into Japan about 1540AD by Dutch traders. But the Japanese showed little initiative in developing firearms, and it was not until the Shogun rule was overthrown that anything was done to establish an indigenous arms industry. In the latter half of the nineteenth century however, more guns were imported and private armament firms sprang up. With the restoration of the Meiji dynasty these firms were bought up in order that all weapons should become standardised. Realising that Japan was well behind Europe in weapon design, the Japanese government of the day initially confined production to copies of the best weapons they could buy from abroad. As time passed these copies were modified and improved and by 1940 Japanese weapons designers had both the experience and the power of original development. Nevertheless many Japanese weapons — artillery and small arms — as well as army organisation and tactical doctrines reflect the influence of German military instructors and advisers imported before World War I.

Designation and Markings
Before discussing the actual weapons of the Japanese infantry it is desirable first to describe the methods used by the Japanese in naming their stores; since only by an understanding of this nomenclature can their weapons be properly identified.

Until defeat at the end of the war brought a change in the system, Japanese Government stores were dated by an artificial time period known as a *Nengo*, which usually commemorated a national or political event. Prior to the accession in 1868 of the Emperor Meiji, for instance, years were reckoned in the *Jimmu nengo*. This dated from the mythological dawn of Japanese history in 660BC, and thus 1945 was the year 2605. Beginning with the first year of Meiji's reign, an alternative method of dating the years was adopted, and *nengos* then corresponded to the reigns of different emperors as follows:

Meiji: from 1868 to 1912
Taisho: from 1912 to 1926
Showa: from 1926 to 1945

Consequently 1945, in addition to being referred to as the year 2605, was also known as *Showa 20*. When using the *Jimmu nengo* it was usual to write only the last two figures of the year, and not to include the word *Jimmu*. Thus 1938 was customarily written as year 98. When using the other *nengo*, however, it is obvious that their names were necessary.

In some cases a specific piece of equipment would be linked with another name (eg Arisaka 90). This was done as a form of recognition to somebody who was closely related to the development of the equipment concerned, and in this case refers to Lieutenant-General Arisaka. (The 90 indicates the year 1930).

Months and days were indicated by the appropriate number of the month or day — there being 12 months in a Japanese year and seven days in a week as in most countries. (Sometimes the Western system of dates is used, such as 2.10.1944 for 2 October 1944).

A list of the characters encountered in the nomenclature of Japanese wartime stores is reproduced at Appendix 4.

Small Arms Ammunition

Rifles, carbines and most Japanese light machine guns, encountered during World War II operations were of 6.5mm (.256in) calibre, and fired the same semi-rimmed cartridge. The latter had an abrupt shoulder and measured 2.98 inches overall. The bullet was of lead-antimony, with a cupro-nickel jacket, and was seated almost a quarter of its even 1¼in length into the cartridge case. Despite copper and tin shortages there was never any general shortage of small arms ammunition possibly because the waning copper supply was given a boost in 1940 when eight million one-sen pieces were taken out of circulation and replaced by aluminium coins. The 6.5mm ammunition was packed in wooden boxes, in Mauser type clips in separate cardboard folds, or with three clips packed together. (The latter was for convenience in loading the conventional 30 and 60 round Japanese cartridge pouches). Other 7.7mm ammunition for the 7.7mm medium and heavy machine guns was usually packed in cloth protected 30-round strips.

First line ammunition for immediate use was carried in bandoliers and in the leather (or rubber substitute) regulation Japanese cartridge pouches worn by all Japanese infantrymen — three pouches per individual. Two of these pouches were of 30-round capacity, and worn in front of the belt on either side of the buckle. The third, which could contain 60 rounds, was worn at the back of the belt. This arrangement enabled the individual infantryman to carry up to 120 rounds in action. When the pouches were filled to capacity however, they were bulky, and invariably caused difficulty when crawling, creeping or moving through cover.

The packaging and storage of Japanese ammunition was generally poor. Even in the damp and humid climate of the Pacific Islands and South-East Asia ammunition boxes were not hermetically sealed, and waxed cardboard or waterproof paper wrappings were rarely used. Packing cases were usually well constructed, but ill-fitting lids permitted depredation by moisture and white ants, and the result was that ammunition stored for any appreciable time became corroded. As many of the rounds were imperfectly turned

Nomenclature of Ammunition associated with individual Japanese weapons

Weapon	*Ammunition*
6.35mm Type 2 (1942) 'Baby' Nambu Pistol	Ball: Type 2 Pistol
8mm Type 14 (1925) Pistol	
8mm Type Nambu Pistol	8mm Hachi Ball
8mm Type 94 Pistol	
8mm Type 100 Sub-Machine Gun	
9mm Type 26 (1893) Revolver	9mm Hachi Ball
6.5mm Type 38 (1905) Long, Medium and Short Rifles	Standard: Ogival Ball
6.5mm Type 3 (1914) Medium Machine Gun	Spitzer Ball (Armour-Piercing
6.5mm Type 44 (1911) Carbine (Cavalry Model)	Ball)
6.5mm Type 96 (1936) Light Machine Gun	Explosive
6.5mm Type 97 (1937) Sniper's Rifle	
6.5mm Type 11 (1922) Light Machine Gun (Nambu)	Wooden Ball (Used for launching
6.5mm Type 91 (1931) Tank Machine Gun (Nambu)	grenades from Type 38 Rifle and Carbine)
6.5mm Type 38 (1905) Carbine (Infantry Model)	
7.7mm Type 92 (1932) Medium Machine Gun	Standard Ball Armour-Piercing (AP)
7.7mm Type 97 (1937) Tank Machine Gun	Tracer (T)
7.7mm Type 99 (1939) Light Machine Gun	Explosive
7.7mm Type 99 (1939) Rifle	AP/T
7.7mm Type 02 (1942) Paratrooper's Rifle	Incendiary/Tracer
7.7mm Type 01 (1942) Medium Machine Gun	
7.7mm Type 99 (1939) Paratrooper's Rifle	
20mm Type 97 (1937) Anti-Tank Rifle	Armour-Piercing and Explosive

In addition to the ammunition for native weapons, Japanese 7.92mm SAA was manufactured for the captured 7.92mm BRNO, 2B (1925) machine guns of Czech and Chinese origin with which some Japanese units were equipped. Such ammunition — Ball, Armour-Piercing and Armour- Piercing/Tracer — was a close copy of the German types.

anyway, the incidence of misfires and other malfunctions was considerably higher than with equivalent American, British or German weapons.

Most Japanese small arms ammunition was unmarked; rounds were recognised by the containers or by their size and shape. On the cartridge heads usually the only markings were primer-crimp stampings in the form of punch marks. And, as the use of a punch tends to mutilate the cartridge head, the headspace chambering and loading of Japanese ammunition inevitably suffered. In appearance the punch marks were short line indentations, usually three in number, radiating out from the primer pocket, with their inner points leaning in to lock the primer in its seat. By Western engineering standards this was a crude arrangement. Lacquered markings which sometimes appeared on the cartridges, were used to distinguish ball, tracer, and armour piercing ammunition. The colour code of such markings was as follows:

Standard Ball:	Red
Tracer:	Green
Armour Piercing:	Black

Rifles

Most of the rifles used by the Japanese were almost entirely made up of the types commonly referred to as the 'Arisaka' rifles. These were the various models normally issued to the Japanese infantry. However, a great variety of rifles was reported as being in use in almost every theatre, and this can be attributed to Japanese reluctance to discard captured material — regardless of its uselessness or that no ammunition was available. Also because they captured large quantities of foreign weapons in the early stages of the war, the Japanese manufactured ammunition in their own factories. On Guadalcanal, for example, large quantities of British, Dutch and American rifles were recaptured. But such weapons were not the normal Japanese issue.

The old-fashioned Meiji 38 was the standard infantry weapon of the Japanese Army throughout World War II. Evolved from the 6.5mm Meiji 30, it was substantially the same weapon as that used throughout the Russo-Japanese War. Basically the Meiji 38 was a copy of the old well-proven German bolt-action Mauser of 1898. Because of its length, 50¼in, and its weight the Meiji 38 was an unwieldy and awkward weapon — especially in jungle terrain. Other shortcomings included the clumsy bolt-head safety, equally clumsy straight bolt-handle, lack of a magazine cut-off, and a back sight without windage or drift compensation. It was reasonably accurate up to 600 yards and had only a slight recoil. A unique feature was the sliding dust cover over the bolt; this protected the working parts from mud and dirt but tended to make the rifle even more awkward to handle. The tangent back sight was of a conventional design and calibrated from 400m to 2,400m in 100m stages. The sights themselves were ordinary barleycorn and open V. To economise in wood the Japanese made the butts in two pieces, from a blank only half as deep as is necessary for a one-piece butt. The rifle sling was used only to carry the rifle, and in a

Above left: The 7.7mm Type 99 rifle. Similar to earlier Japanese rifles but in .303in calibre. Note the folding monopod.

Above centre: The ever popular Arisaka 6.5mm Meiji 38.

Above right: The Meiji 38 'Short'; the shortened version of the Arisaka.

prone position Japanese soldiers were taught to fire by grasping the rifle with their left hand just in front of the trigger guard and aim with the sling hanging loose and so without using it to steady the weapon. Rapid fire, as practised in the British Army with the bolt action Lee Enfield rifle, was virtually impossible with the Meiji 38 because the slack sling and the action, cocking on the closing of the bolt, made it difficult for the physically small Japanese soldier to hold the Meiji in to his shoulder while operating the bolt.

Specification of the Meiji 38

Calibre	6.5mm (.256in)
Length	50.25in. With bayonet 65.5in
Weight	9lb (without bayonet)
Barrel length	31.4in
Action	Modified Mauser type
Bolt	One piece rotating — two front locking lugs
Bolt retainer	Mauser type
Extractor	Non-rotating long spring claw (no supporting rib on bolt)
Ejector	Rocker type — left side
Feed	Mauser type — five rounds
Holding open device	Rising platform of magazine
Rifling	Four grooves RH Concentric
Sights, front	Barleycorn
back	Tangent. Graduated 400-2,400m with battle sight for use below 400m
Sighting radius	27.25in
Sling	Underneath
Stock	One piece (Two-piece butt)
Stocking up	Mauser practice
Handguards	Rear only
Safety, mechanical	British No 3 Rifle type
applied	Special
Trigger action	Two pulls. British No 3 Rifle type
Special features	Applied safety
	Dust cover
	Bolt stop lug on bolt
	Butt made from two pieces of wood
Muzzle velocity	2,400 feet/sec (2,690 feet/sec)
Wt of round	324gr
Wt of bullet	137.7gr
Wt of propellant	34gr

Although it was a Mauser type rifle, the Meiji 38 — like its Japanese predecessors — possessed certain features which were not normally found on the conventional Mauser. For example on the Meiji there was no rear locking lug on the bolt, and an extra lug was machined behind the top

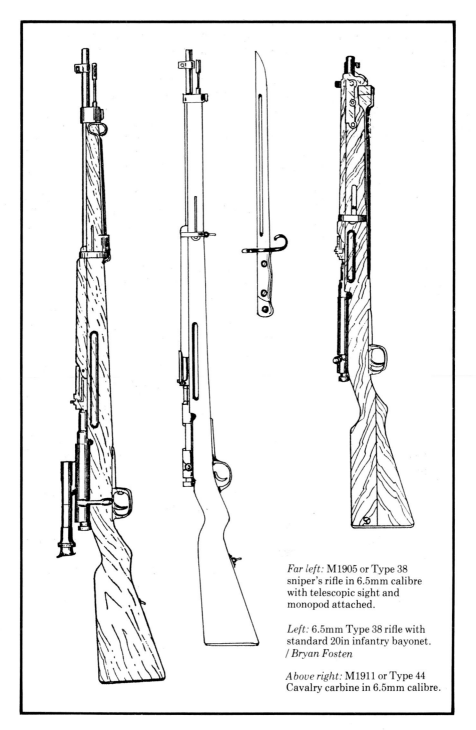

Far left: M1905 or Type 38
sniper's rifle in 6.5mm calibre
with telescopic sight and
monopod attached.

Left: 6.5mm Type 38 rifle with
standard 20in infantry bayonet.
/ *Bryan Fosten*

Above right: M1911 or Type 44
Cavalry carbine in 6.5mm calibre.

locking lug; this acted as a bolt stop as well as an actuator for the rocker type ejector. Nor was there a support on the bolt for the extractor, and the extractor itself was larger than on the German Gewehr 98.

The two recesses cut in the bolt to accommodate the safety stud of the sear were similar to the arrangement of the British No 3 Rifle type trigger mechanism. Similarly the two cam grooves were also reminiscent of the British No 1 Rifle, and — as the cocking piece went right back into the slot in the bolt plug when the rifle was cocked — it was readily apparent that the action was cocked on closing the bolt and not by simply raising the bolt lever. Finally the bolt plug, which incorporated the applied safety mechanism, was totally different.

Another important difference relates to the applied safety mechanism which in the Meiji could only be applied in the cocked position. A bolt plug was keyed to the bolt and also to the striker. On pushing the bolt plug in and rotating it clockwise about 40°, the striker was also rotated and its bent (cocking piece) was turned away from the sear to a position behind a step in the body. At the same time a shoulder on the bolt plug rotated to lie alongside a lug on the bolt so that the bolt could be rotated without rotating the plug. The plug was prevented from turning by a tang on its underside being rotated into a bayonet slot in the body. To counter-rotate the bolt plug, it had first to be pushed in again, in order to disengage the tang from this bayonet slot. The striker spring acted as a spring for the plug.

The 6.5mm Meiji 38 was the Imperial Japanese Army's basic rifle, and all the other Japanese rifles described in the following pages were evolved from it or were fore-runners of it. It was the most extensively used Japanese weapon of World War II, and although it was superseded by later models of a different calibre, it remained popular with the troops. After the war Japanese soldiers expressed a muted preference for the old reliable Arisaka 6.5 over any of the later Japanese rifles and all foreign weapons, with the exception of the American Garand. In spite of its shortcomings the Meiji 38 proved to be a good reliable combat rifle and it was responsible for the deaths of many thousands of Allied soldiers who were armed with the best weapons in the world.

After the 'Long' 38 the Meiji 38 'Short' rifle was probably the most common of the Arisaka models. Except that the overall length was reduced by approximately six inches this weapon was identical with the 'Long'. Cutting down the barrel resulted in reduction in weight of one pound, but the advantage of a long barrel — in reducing muzzle blast and flash — was lost. Most Meiji 38 'Shorts' were issued to units other than infantry; the specification for the Meiji 38 'Short' follows:

Calibre	6.5mm
Length	44.5in
Weight	8.5lb
Barrel length	25.5in
Sights	as 'Long' rifle

Like the Meiji 'Short' the Meiji 38 carbine was also identical with the Meiji 38 'Long' rifle, except that its overall length was reduced by approximately 12in, so cutting the weight to 7¾lb. Other differences are that the sling of this weapon was fitted to the left side and the muzzle velocity is less. Its specification follows:

Calibre	6.5mm
Length	38in
Weight	7.75lb
Barrel length	19in
Sights	As 'Long' rifle, but graduated to 2,000m only

The Meiji 44 Carbine was originally designed for use by cavalry. But its short length and the fact that it had a permanently attached folding bayonet meant that it was not necessary for a soldier to have a long bayonet scabbard attached to his belt, made it popular among Japanese infantry engaged in jungle operations. From its butt to the lower band, the Meiji 44 was almost exactly the same as the Meiji 38 carbine. Between these two points the only differences amounted to a trap in the butt to carry a cleaning rod; and a groove in the stock below the upper band to house the last few inches of the bayonet when it was folded back. To accommodate the bayonet the muzzle was modified, the fore sight being moved back three inches to allow a steel cap to be fitted to the muzzle. This cap carried the hinge and locking arrangement for the triangular shaped poniard type bayonet. The bayonet had a blade length of 14in, and its latch mechanism was a masterpiece of ruggedness and dependability. However the overall weight of bayonet and muzzle cap tended to throw the carbine completely out of balance — making it muzzle heavy and difficult to aim. Another major disadvantage accrued from the fact that the bayonet could not be detached to serve as a knife. The Meiji 44 Carbine's specification follows:

Calibre	6.5mm
Length	38.25in
Weight	8.75lb
Barrel length	19.25in
Sights	As Meiji 38 Carbine (up to 2,000m)
Muzzle velocity	2,460 feet/sec

The Meiji 38 6.5mm Sniper Rifle was simply a Meiji 38 'Long' rifle fitted with a telescopic sight and a folding monopod. The only modification was that the bolt lever was bent down in order to prevent it fouling the sight. The telescopic sight was short, having an overall length of some 6⅞in excluding the rubber eyepiece; with the rubber eyepiece it measured 1¼in more.

The sight was mounted well back on the rifle, in order to cater for the generally short necks of Japanese soldiers, and because the glass had a very short eye relief (less than 1¾in), it was mounted off-centre — to the left —

to permit easier loading and movement of the bolt without the need for major modification of either the bolt or the receiver.

The telescopic sight itself was rugged and practical, but it had few exceptional features to commend it. The reticule was a simple three lines, graduated vertically in range settings and graduated horizontally for windage or lead. The rifle was calibrated on 300 metres; all other ranges had to be held over or under. One good feature worthy of mention is that the telescope was efficiently waterproofed — its lens being firmly sealed and heavily protected from both moisture and shock by the rigid close-fitting tube assembly. The result was that it was capable of withstanding trying conditions of humidity and changing temperature encountered in jungle terrain. The Meiji 38 Sniper Rifle's specification follows:

Calibre	6.5mm
Length	50.25in
Weight	10.5lb with sight
Barrel length	31.4in
Sight	2.5 magnification, 10° field of view

Finally, before leaving the Meiji 38 family of rifles, a brief review of its forerunners and their history may be worth while as some of the early models were issued to garrison troops and militia units raised in metropolitan Japan towards the end of the war. Developed from the French Chassepot in the 1880s the original Meiji 13 rifle of 11mm calibre — named after its designer Major Murata — was virtually only a modified Chassepot. This rifle was first modified to bring it in line with the Gras (metal cartridge case instead of a paper one) and then fitted with a magazine. In this new guise the Meiji 13 was renamed the Meiji 22, and although a 'new' 8mm Japanese rifle, the Meiji 20, had been introduced two years previously — the calibre remained 11mm.

The Meiji 30 rifle was designed in 1897. (Credit for the new design has been attributed to both Major Murata and Colonel Arisaka, the officer who headed a commission of inquiry into weapons used in the Sino-Japanese war. In the event it was Arisaka's name which stuck to the series). The new weapon, a modified Mauser, was of an even smaller calibre than the Meiji 20, being 6.5mm — the smallest service rifle ever known to have been adopted until long after World War II. A Meiji 30 carbine, identical in all respects to the rifle except for a shorter barrel length, followed and both weapons were used throughout the Russo-Japanese War. Then, as a result of experience gained during fighting in Manchuria where it had been found necessary to have a dust cover for the actions of rifles, the Meiji 38 was evolved.

The main difference between the Type 99 and the Meiji series of rifles was the increased calibre of 7.7mm. The length of this rifle was approximately the same as the Meiji 38 Short Rifle — as in fact were all the subsequent rifles introduced, and this lends credence to the view that the extra length of the Meiji 38 was offset by considerations of weight and unwieldiness in jungle conditions.

Above: Japanese rifles and their Allied counterparts in World War II. Left to right: 1 6.5mm Arisaka 38; 2 US .30MI semi-automatic carbine; 3 Mosin-Nagant; 4 .303in British SMLE Mk3; 5 7.92mm German Gewehr 98/40; 6 7.7m (.303in) Type 99 Arisaka.

Other differences were mainly additional. The monopod of the Meiji 38 sniper's rifle (Type 97) was retained and the back sight had two 'lead-off' arms fitted to it for anti-aircraft use. The back sight remained in the same position but instead of the V notch, it had an aperture of approximately $\frac{1}{8}$in diameter. The sight was graduated up to 1,500 metres only, but it was long enough to give a deflection of up to 2,000 metres. The bayonet was the type fitted on the old Meiji 30. Minor differences included a different type of nose cap, hinged magazine bottom plate, and sling on left side. In general, the finish was inferior to that of the previous rifles. The Type 99's specification follows:

Calibre	7.7mm
Length	44in
Weight	8.25lb
Barrel length	27.25in (25.25in)
Sights, front	Barleycorn
back	Tangent. Aperture 300-1,500m and battle sight
Muzzle velocity	2,390 feet/sec
Wt of round	417gr
Wt of bullet	189gr
Wt of propellant	41gr

To facilitate production of this rifle in the latter stages of the war certain modifications were introduced. These included: leaving off the monopod, omitting the lead arms, a cylindrical bolt knob (in place of the earlier oval one) and inferior quality furniture. (It is relevant to note that Italian technicians were employed in Japanese arsenals from about 1850. As a result, Italian arms manufacturers made occasional weapons for Japan).

The most predominant of the extraneous rifles encountered in World War II, however, was the 6.5mm Meiji 30, to which reference — as predecessor to the Meiji 38 — has been made earlier. Its characteristics are listed below:

Calibre	6.5mm
Length	50.2in
Weight	8.5lb
Barrel length	31.25in
Feed	5-rd Mauser type magazine
Applied safety	Catch on bolt head applicable in cocked position only by pulling back and rotating ¼ turn clockwise
Mechanical safety	Mauser
Stock	One piece (butt with separate spliced toe) No front handguard
Sights, front	Blade
back	Tangent
Sighting radius	approx 28in
Sling	On underside
Muzzle velocity	2,380 feet/sec
Wt of bullet	162gr
Wt of propellant	33gr

For use by paratroops, a special break-down model of the Type 99 rifle was developed. In both this and the Type 2 described below, the rifles were broken at the barrel-body joint — something of an unusual feature in service rifles. In the Type 99, there were interrupted threads and a spring loaded plunger as a securing catch; the only other difference was that the bolt lever was detachable. In general, the standard of workmanship in this rifle was poor. Its weight was 8.75lb and all other details corresponded to the Type 99.

The later model of the parachutist 99 rifle, known as Type 2, was superior in as much as the design of the takedown lock as sound and very strong. It consisted of a key and socket joint secured by a transverse locking bolt. The bolt lever was not removable, but the lead-off sight bars and the monopod were omitted. This rifle weighed 9lb but was in other respects as for the earlier model.

Reference has already been made to the fact that American weapons — captured rifles — were used by the Japanese.* Other Japanese rifles were occasionally found in the standard 6.5mm calibre, stamped 'Beretta'. Such rifles had Italian 1891 type receivers and bolts — the receivers being modified for Mauser type magazines, but otherwise the weapons conformed to standard Japanese design.

Pistols and Revolvers

Officers, NCOs, 'service' troops such as drivers, clerks, orderlies and the like, tank and cavalrymen as well as members of Japan's para-military forces and gendarmerie were issued with revolvers or pistols. Such weapons seem to have been prestige symbols, and they were usually carried in well made leather holsters with belt-loops and shoulder straps. Nambu 8mm pistols of 1925 and 1939 vintage predominated but many second line and para-military units were issued with old Meiji 26 revolvers. Introduced in 1893 this handgun is similar in external appearance to early Smith and Wesson revolvers. Originally a cavalry weapon, the Meiji 26 is double action only and in the original design provision was made for the attachment of a wooden shoulder stock. Its specification follows:

Calibre	9mm
Weight	2.25lb. Rather heavy for a revolver of this calibre
Length of barrel	4.69in
Cylinder	6 chambered
Sights, front	Detachable blade
back	Groove in barrel strap

The external appearance of the earliest models of the self-loading 8mm Nambu pistol closely resemble the German P.08 Luger Parabellum, although the locking action is that of the Mauser. Its specification follows:

---

* Details of these are recorded in *German Infantry Weapons of World War II* and *British and American Infantry Weapons of World War II* by the author, published by Arms and Armour Press, London, and Arco, New York.

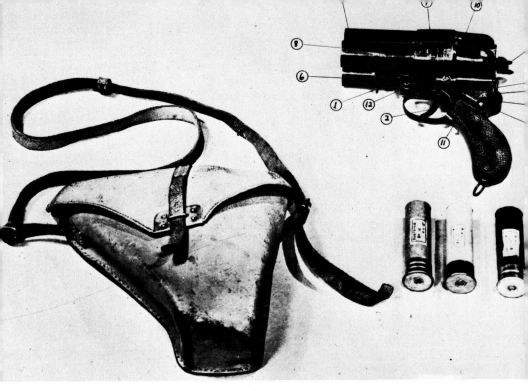

Above: Signal pistol. Similar in design and function to the British 'Verey' pistol. / *IWM*

Right: The popular Nambu 8mm self loading pistol. Similar in appearance to the P.08 Luger Parabellum. Locking action resembles the Mauser. / *IWM*

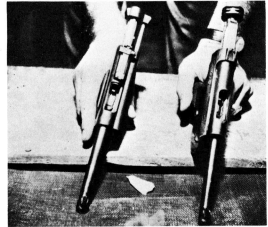

Calibre	8mm
Length of barrel	4.69in
Length overall	8.25in
Weight	1lb 15oz
Sights, front	Blade, adjustable laterally
back	'U' notch at rear of body. Some models have an adjustable rear sight for use in conjunction with detachable butt stock
Ammunition	8mm with necked case, similar in shape to 7.65mm Parabellum cartridge

The Taisho 14 8mm pistol was a modified form of the early Nambu, in which the safety grip was replaced by a safety lever fitted to left side of body. When it is rotated rearwards, this lever prevents movement of sear and slide. Some models of this pistol had an enlarged trigger guard to clear a gloved finger. Its specifications are listed below:

Calibre	8mm
Length of barrel	4.25in
Length overall	9in
Weight	1lb 14.5oz

The Type 94 pistol was first produced in 1934 for the Japanese export market, and Japanese catalogues listed it for sale before the war. It was a well balanced weapon, but of poor design and inferior workmanship. The magazine held six rounds; the sights were crude — seldom having more than a very rough relationship to the axis of the bore.

Finally, what was undoubtedly the best designed and best finished of all Japanese hand guns, the so-called 'Baby Nambu' — a self-loading pistol of 7mm calibre and six round magazine capacity, which was issued only to officers. Weighing less than one and a half pounds and having a barrel length of about 3¹/₈in the Baby Nambu could be stripped and reassembled without the use of tools. This pistol was highly prized as a souvenir by American servicemen who are said to have paid up to $200 or two bottles of whisky for a Baby Nambu.

Sub-Machine Guns
Apart from a few captured weapons, the Japanese used five types of sub-machine gun during World War II. Of these, two were very similar to their German and Swiss counterparts — the 9mm Schmeisser (German MP 40) and the Steyr-Solothurn (German MP 28) both of which were bought by the Japanese in large quantities before the war. The other three types were different models of the same basic design, which — though of Japanese origin — closely followed the Steyr-Solothurn pattern.

Characteristics of the 9mm German MP 40 (Schmeisser)
Length	31.5in
Weight	9.5lb

Above: The Type 100 8mm sub-machine gun. This model, made at Tokyo Arsenal, was similar in shape to the German Schmeisser.

Below: Jap 20mm anti-tank gun.

Rate of Fire	500rpm
Type of Fire	Auto and semi-auto
Sights, front	Barleycorn. Adjustable laterally
back	Tangent with 'V' notch. Graduated 100-1,000m

Characteristics of the 7.63mm Swiss Steyr-Solothurn

Length	31.25in
Weight	92.5lb
Rate of Fire	700rpm
Type of Fire	Auto and semi-auto
Sights, front	Barleycorn. Adjustable laterally
back	Graduated 100-500m

The three Japanese weapons were all known as Type 100, and designed to fire the 8mm pistol cartridge. All worked on the case-projection principle, all were distinguished by a perforated barrel casing, and all had the cocking handle on the right with usual Japanese egg-shaped knob. In each model provision was made for the Type 30 Bayonet, to fit on a tube under the barrel casing.

Individual models were known as the Army, the Naval Parachutists' SMG, and the Simplified model; despite this nomenclature all three were issued to army units.

The Army model was manufactured at Tokyo Arsenal, had a one piece wooden stock, similar in shape to that of the German Schmeisser and it was fitted with a 30-round curved box type magazine. Other specifications were as follows:

Length	36in
Weight	10lb
Rate of Fire	450rpm
Type of Fire	Automatic only
Sights, front	Barleycorn
back	Radial with aperture graduated from 100-1,500m

The Naval Parachutists model of the Type 100 was made at Nagaya and except that it had a folding butt it was the same weapon as the Army model. Only the Simplified model was really different. With this weapon the bipod was omitted and the bayonet fitting was a simple stud on barrel casing. Much was done to reduce the weight and a simple muzzle brake-cum-compensator was fitted.

Length	36in
Weight	9lb 2oz (including sling and magazine, which weighs 9oz)
Rate of Fire	Estimated to be over 800rpm
Sights, front	Barleycorn
back	Fixed, with 'V' notch and aperture

Anti-Tank Rifles

Japanese anti-tank tactics and anti-vehicle measures were concerned more with the employment of explosive charges, mines and grenades rather than anti-tank guns and rifles. But the 20mm anti-tank rifle, rare though it was, deserves mention as an interesting weapon. Known as the Type 97 Anti-Tank Rifle this weapon was air-cooled, gas-operated and magazine fed; it was mounted on a bipod and controlled from the shoulder with the assistance of a monopod fitted to the butt. The shoulder piece was padded and a muzzle brake was fitted. As an anti-tank weapon it was obsolete by 1941. Its characteristics were as follows:

Length	89.5in
Weight	150lb
Feed	Detachable box magazine holding 7 rounds

Machine Guns

Light Machine Guns

In combat the Japanese infantry platoon was normally divided into six groups (each of eight men at full establishment) and three of these groups would be armed with light machine guns. The standard LMG throughout the war was the Type 96 6.5mm Nambu, and this weapon probably caused more Allied casualties in the SW Pacific and Burma than any other Japanese weapon.

Brought out in 1936, the Type 96 — or 'Nambu Light' as it was known to a generation of US Servicemen — was similar to the British Bren in external appearance. Like its predecessor, the Taisho II, it was gas-operated and air-cooled, but unlike its predecessor it had a detachable box magazine feed. Its specifications were as follows:

Length	42in
Weight	18.5lb
Rate of Fire	550rpm
Type of Fire	Automatic only
Sights, front	Barleycorn
back	Drum controlled aperture (as Bren). Graduated in 100s of metres from 2-1,600m. A windgauge was fitted
Feed	30-round box magazine on top of the gun

Some units, particularly in China, were equipped with the older Taisho II forerunner of the Nambu Light. This was a gas-operated and air-cooled machine gun designed on the French Hotchkiss principle, having a heavy jacket on the barrel on which were cut radial fins to assist cooling.

The gun was fitted with a unique cartridge feed, which — while theoretically sound — did not work well in practice.

A hopper on the left side of the gun could be loaded with six clips of five rounds, each held in position by means of a spring-loaded follower. Rounds were fed from the clip by the feed mechanism, sideways to a position in front of the breech block, and during this movement each round was oiled. Its specifications were as follows:

Top: 6.5mm light machine gun, Taisho 11. Gas operated, air cooled.

Above left: 7.7mm light machine gun M99 very similar to the Type 96 6.5mm model. / *IWM*

Above: Breech block of the 7.7mm medium machine gun M92. / *IWM*

Left: Type 92 heavy machine gun.

Length	43.5in
Weight	22.5lb
Rate of Fire	500rpm
Type of Fire	Automatic only
Sights, front	Barleycorn
back	'V' radial. 300-1,500m

In more common use towards the end of the war was the Type 99 7.7mm LMG — a weapon similar in design to the Type 96. Its characteristics follow:

Length	42in
Weight	20lb
Rate of Fire	500rpm
Type of Fire	Automatic only
Sights, front	Flat post
back	Drum type aperture, fitted with windgauge
	Graduated 200-1,500m

The feed, safety and method of operation was exactly the same as for the Type 98 and the structural differences resulted entirely from the increase in calibre.

Other LMGs included the Type 99 7.7mm Parachutists' Model, which were merely a lightened version of the Type 99, with a detachable butt and folding pistol grip. The Type 97 7.7mm LMG was designed in the first place for fighting vehicles, but Japanese infantry in the SW Pacific used the weapon fitted with a bipod and with the armour jacket removed. Its specification was as follows:

Length	46in
Weight	26lb
Rate of Fire	500rpm
Type of Fire	Automatic only
Sights, front	Blade
back	Drum type aperture. Graduated 200-1,500m

A 20-round box magazine was normally used with this gun although a 30-round magazine was designed specifically for use with this gun in its ground role.

ZB 26 (Czech) LMGs in 7.92mm calibre of Czech and Chinese manufacture also saw service with the Japanese Army. Originally manufactured in Czechoslovakia the ZB 26 was sold around the world in the 1930s and subsequently manufactured in Chinese arsenals. Being the forerunner of the Bren the ZB 26 possessed most of the features of the British weapon, although there are certain differences such as a longer piston consequent on the gas vent being nearer the muzzle, and the barrel finned for cooling purposes.

Length	46in
Weight	19.5lb
Rate of Fire	600rpm
Type of Fire	Single shot and automatic
Sights, front	Blade
back	Drum type aperture, graduated 200-1,500m
Feed	Detachable box magazine, 20 rounds

The Japanese gun fired 7.92mm rimless ammunition and as this ammunition was not standard for the Japanese, its provision exacerbated supply problems in the field.

Medium Machine Guns
The regular Japanese medium machine gun was the Taisho 3 a 1914 Hotchkiss type, 6.5mm calibre, gas operated, air cooled and strip fed. Eight of these weapons or the alternative Type 92 7.7m gun were issued to a machine gun company.

The 7.7mm Type 92 was copied from the Taisho 3 and thus, apart from the larger calibre, there are only slight differences — such as the traversing handles in the Taisho 3 being fixed in a vertical position and the back sight graduated from 3-2,200 instead of 2,700 metres as is the case with the Type 92. In both guns the firing mechanism was at the rear, like the British Vickers or American .50 Browning. The Taisho 3 MMG's specifications were as follows:

Calibre	6.5mm
Length	47in
Weight	60lb (67lb)
Rate of Fire	400-500rpm
Type of Fire	Automatic only
Mounting	67lb weight, 33.5° traverse, from −15° to + 9° elevation

Specifications of the Type 92 MMG

Calibre	7.7mm
Length	46in
Weight	63lb
Rate of Fire	450rpm
Type of Fire	Automatic only
Sights, front	Barleycorn
back	Tangent aperture. For indirect fire a dial sight was used, and in the AA role a ring foresight and 'U' back sight were fitted
Mounting	Tripod, weighing 60lb; allowing 33.5° traverse with from −15° to +11° elevation closely resembling that of the Taisho 3. It could be fitted with two carrying handles or two wheels for transport and had a AA extension

The Type I 7.7mm medium machine gun which came into service late in the war, was simply a lighter version of the Type 92. Like its predecessors it was gas operated on the Hotchkiss principle, strip feed and air-cooled. One noteworthy feature was that the tripod mounting weighed only 36.5lb and gave an extended traverse of 45°. The Type I MMG's specification follows:

Length	38in (without flash hider)
Weight	33.5lb
Rate of Fire	Over 450rpm

Heavy Machine Guns
Heavy machine guns were not included in the infantry organisation, but a brief reference to them is included here because they are categorised as small arms. In effect such weapons were used by the Japanese in anti-aircraft or anti-tank roles. 13.2mm Type 93 and 20mm Type 98 guns predominated, but the Japanese also had a 13mm Vickers type weapon — similar in design and appearance to the British Vickers .5in.

The Type 93 13.2mm HMG was a gas operated, air cooled and magazine fed weapon. It was normally mounted singly on a light tripod; alternatively two guns could be mounted together on a heavier carriage with elevating and traversing gears. On this latter mounting, all round traverse was obtainable and elevation from 0-85°. Its characteristics were as follows:

Length	89in
Weight	87lb
Rate of Fire	450rpm
Type of Fire	Automatic only
Sights	The twin mounting had a course and speed sight incorporated
MV	Ball 2,210 feet/sec
	AP 2,280 feet/sec

The Type 98 20mm HMG was also a gas-operated, magazine fed weapon. But it was mounted on a wheeled carriage giving it an all-round traverse. The carriage had detachable wooden wheels and a split trail. Two sets of recoil springs were fitted to the carriage, which were adjustable. Run-out was cushioned by means of an air cylinder and valves. Its specifications were as follows:

Weight of gun and carriage	836lb
Length of barrel	57in
Rate of Fire	120rpm
Type of Fire	Automatic only
MV	2,720 feet/sec
Mounting	Traverse 360°
	Elevation −10 to + 85°

Colonel in M1938 blouse.   Lieutenant in M1930 blouse.

Lieutenant-Colonel in Tropical blouse.　　　　Sergeant in tank overalls.

Corporal in M1930 blouse.   Japanese Infantryman 1942.

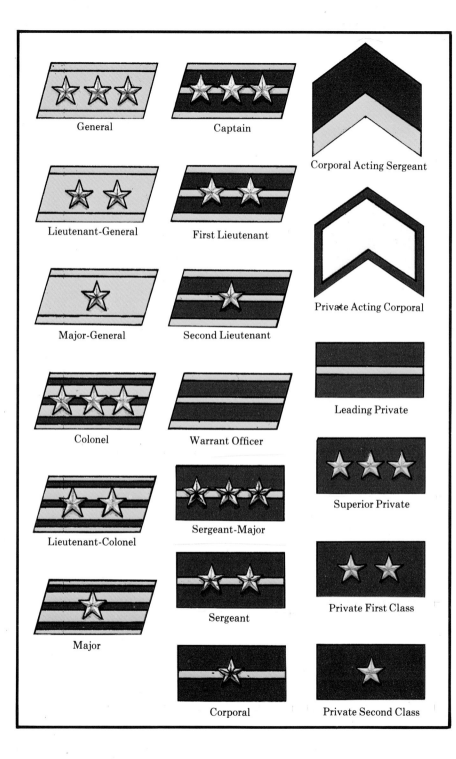

General

Captain

Corporal Acting Sergeant

Lieutenant-General

First Lieutenant

Private Acting Corporal

Major-General

Second Lieutenant

Leading Private

Colonel

Warrant Officer

Superior Private

Lieutenant-Colonel

Sergeant-Major

Private First Class

Major

Sergeant

Corporal

Private Second Class

Miscellaneous Guns
Before leaving the subject of machine guns mention must be made of one other such weapon used by the Japanese in reasonable quantities. This was the so-called 'Type 92 Lewis 7.7mm' medium machine gun — a British designed weapon classed by the British as a *light* machine gun, — which the Japanese employed as a medium gun in an anti-aircraft role. The mechanism of the weapon itself was the same as its British counterpart, and such differences as existed between the British and Japanese models were consequent on its different role. Thus the butt was replaced by a spade grip. The Type 92 Lewis's characteristics were as follows:

Length	56in
Weight	26lb
Rate of Fire	600rpm
Type of Fire	Automatic only
Sights, front	Blade
back	Aperture folding leaf. Graduated 0-1,700m

It should be noted that the Japanese Lewis fired standard British ammunition .303.

Bayonets and Swords
The Japanese put great emphasis on the use of cold steel in battle. Japanese infantrymen were taught to consider the bayonet their most essential weapon, their training included many hours of bayonet fighting and by tradition they were expected to use the bayonet effectively in battle. The general issue bayonet weighed 14oz, and had a 15½in long blade. It was a rough, mass-manufactured but sturdy and efficient product, and in action the Japanese infantryman invariably carried his rifle with bayonet fixed.

The big heavy swords carried by Japanese officers were not just badges of rank but for use whenever the opportunity offered. Both the cavalry sabres and the classic single-edged blades of Japan's feudal era were capable of slicing a handkerchief in mid-air or of parting a man's body from collar-bone to waist in a single clean slash. Until the early 1930s it was said that Tokyo's sword makers were the remnants of a dying profession but by 1940 their business was booming.

Grenades
Like the bayonet, the hand grenade was intimately associated with the Japanese soldier in World War II. In the Pacific and in Burma grenades became, on occasions, the only weapons used during night operations by both Japanese and Allied troops. This disproportionate use of what may be regarded as a relatively unsophisticated weapon was caused by two main factors. First, the jungle cover brought opposing troops close to each other, and the grenade is a short range weapon; second, the Japanese put great emphasis on night operations — launching many of their attacks and probing the Allied localities during the hours of darkness. Because no weapon at that time could be accurately aimed in the dark, the grenade

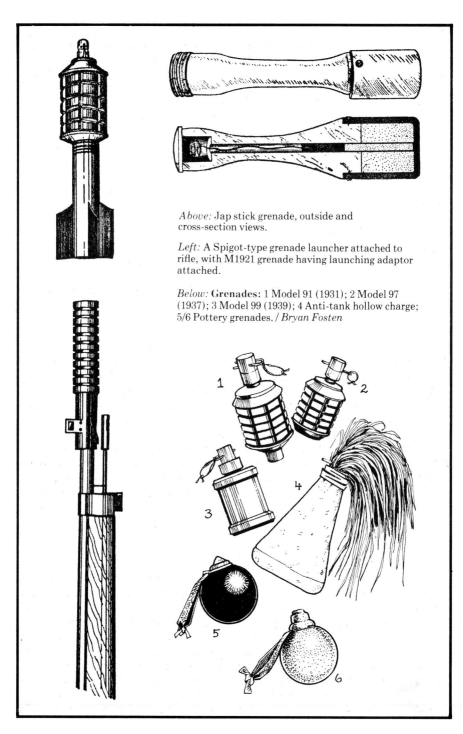

Above: Jap stick grenade, outside and cross-section views.

Left: A Spigot-type grenade launcher attached to rifle, with M1921 grenade having launching adaptor attached.

Below: **Grenades:** 1 Model 91 (1931); 2 Model 97 (1937); 3 Model 99 (1939); 4 Anti-tank hollow charge; 5/6 Pottery grenades. / *Bryan Fosten*

became the accepted means of dealing with targets at close range. As a night weapon it had the advantage that it would not give away the thrower's position as would the flash of a rifle or machine gun.

Almost every Japanese soldier carried grenades; when the situation became desperate many of them used grenades to commit *seppuku* — igniting a grenade by banging it against a helmet and then hugging the spluttering explosives to their chest. Three types of explosive grenade were common. Two were fragmentation weapons similar to the British and American Mills design; the third was a potato masher grenade, which relied on blast rather than fragmentation effect. Of these three types the most effective could be projected from a mortar as well as thrown by hand. Known as the Type 91 (or M1931) grenade its fragmentation was marginally more effective than the second type — the Type 97 (M1937) — which was designed only as a hand grenade. The Type 91 was generally more reliable because it was packed and transported in waterproof containers which protected it from the humid atmosphere and deteriorating effects of the tropics.

The body of the Type 91 was cylindrical, the fuse being contained in a smaller cylinder at the front end. The other end contained a primer and propelling charge which had no function if the weapon was hand-thrown, but which adapted it to its secondary purpose of launching from the Taisho 10 (M1921) or 89 (M1929) grenade dischargers (knee-mortars). This propellant-containing portion would be unscrewed if the grenade was hand-thrown, making it lighter to throw and less bulky to carry.

With the Type 91 the conventional type of Japanese grenade fuse was used. This fuse was in the shape of a long projecting button which was held at 'safe' by a two-shafted crosspin, shaped like a strong hairpin with straight sides. The grenade would be armed by withdrawing this pin — an action which was facilitated by a loop of heavy twine tied to the 'U' of the hairpin. When the grenade was to be thrown, the fuse was ignited by striking the front end of the button against a hard object — usually a helmet. This action drove a firing pin into the fuse percussion cap and initiated the eight-second fuse.

The firing pin mechanism included a lever arrangement whereby it was possible to unscrew the firing pin inside its collar so that its point could not strike the cap. When fired from the launcher, there was no need to strike the endcap or button to start the fuse burning, as an inertia mechanism caused the firing pin to set back against the action of a very weak spring, as the projectile left the barrel. The fuse time of eight seconds remained the same, whether the grenade was hand-thrown or launched.

The Type 97 was identical with the Type 91, but for the fact that it had no provision for launching from a grenade discharger. It had no propellant-container attached to its base and there was no threaded hole provided to permit the attachment of such a device. Otherwise it was the same — an inexpensively-made version of the more versatile Type 91 which could only be thrown. It possessed no advantage over the earlier grenade except ease of manufacture. Its compactness could be matched by the Type 91 by the

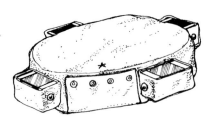

Left and above: Anti-tank mine Type 99. / *Bryan Fosten*

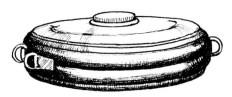

Left and above: An earlier type of anti-tank mine Type 93. / *Bryan Fosten*

Left: Anti-tank mine as used by naval forces.

Below: Anti-personnel mine.

simple expedient of unscrewing and discarding the propellant base. Its explosive effect, of course, was identical with that of the Type 91.

The Japanese stick grenade, which relied for its effect on blast rather than fragmentation, had several functional advantages when compared with the two fragmentation types. Its fuse and arming mechanism was housed in its long wooden handle and was well protected from moisture. It was very handy to throw, especially from a prone position. Finally it had a very short fuse which sparked less than the fragmentation grenades, and so — apart from being less easily detected in flight — such grenades presented less opportunity for getting out of their way.

Smoke grenades were little used by the Japanese and the only one of any consequence was the 50mm grenade illustrated. Like the Type 91 fragmentation grenade this bomb could be projected from a grenade launcher or mortar.

Infantry Mortars

The fact that mortars are simple weapons, easy to operate and maintain, and ideal infantry support weapons in close country was appreciated by the Japanese early in their pre-World War II armament programme. The simplest and smallest of these weapons which was classed as a 'grenade launcher' has already been discussed in the section on grenades.* The original Type 10 (Model 1921) grenade launcher which had a calibre of 50mm, and was smooth-bored, was purely a grenade launcher. But this weapon had largely been replaced at the time of the attack on Pearl Harbor, and its successor, the Type 89 (M1929) 50mm grenade launcher with a rifled barrel, could fire mortar 'shells' up to 700 metres. As such it could be classed as a light mortar, comparable with the British 2-inch platoon weapon or the American 60mm company mortar.

Because the barrel of both weapons rested on a stubby curved baseplate, both the Type 10 and the Type 89 grenade dischargers were mistakenly dubbed 'knee-mortars', although they could not be fired from the knee or the thigh.

The Type 89 weapon weighed about 10½lb and its shells, longer and more streamlined than the grenades, weighed 1¾lb each. Lightness was a common characteristic of most Japanese mortars especially as the weight of the particular weapon was related to the weight of its missile. By designing their mortars to project the heaviest possible missile with the lightest possible charge the Japanese sacrificed range, and often accuracy, for target effect. For jungle warfare, where visibility is extremely limited and accurate obseration of fire was rarely possible, this policy was justified.

Because it was fired by a trigger arrangement (and not by gravity action as was the British 2-inch mortar) the Type 89 could be aimed at nearly all

* The line between a grenade launcher and a mortar is thinly drawn. One concept is that a grenade launcher is merely a means of increasing the distance of grenade projection beyond the limits of throwing by hand, and perhaps also to increase the accuracy of throw. The ammunition for such a weapon must necessarily be grenades. A mortar, on the other hand, is used to increase the weight of the missile as well as the range, throwing a heavier bomb a greater distance and performing a mission beyond the capabilities of a mere grenade launcher.

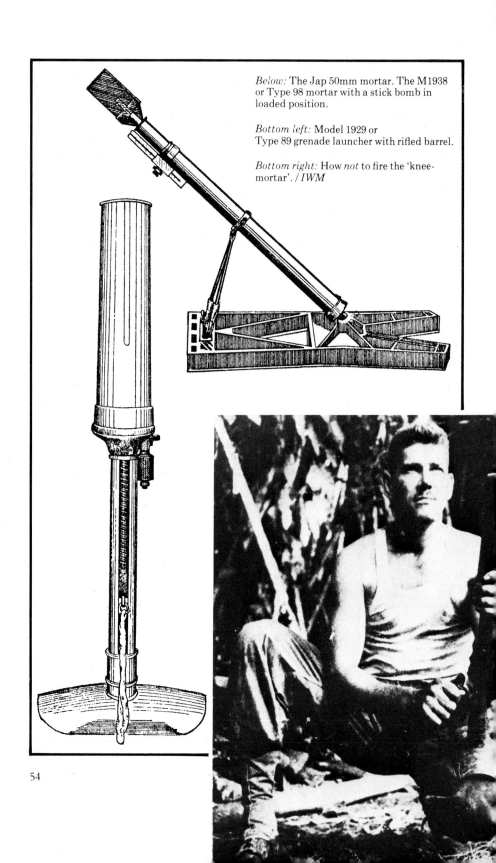

Below: The Jap 50mm mortar. The M1938 or Type 98 mortar with a stick bomb in loaded position.

Bottom left: Model 1929 or Type 89 grenade launcher with rifled barrel.

Bottom right: How *not* to fire the 'knee-mortar'. / *IWM*

angles above the horizontal — the curve of the baseplate allowing a grip on the ground or a log at lower angles of elevation. This grenade launcher, like its predecessor, was designed to be fired normally at an angle of 45°, range being regulated by screwing the barrel up or down to vary the chamber space. However, the Japanese infantrymen sooned learned that their knee-mortar could be fired with the barrel almost flat along the ground and used very effectively to project grenades at very short distances into pillbox and window openings.

In jungle warfare the variable volume chamber as a means of regulating the range has one great advantage over the more usual method of altering the barrel angle. To fire the latter through a ceiling of branches and leaves a suitably sized hole in the jungle canopy is essential. This poses a problem which the Japanese resolved by designing the ammunition for medium and heavy mortars to include a time delay device which prevented the ammunition from becoming armed as soon as it left the barrel. This allowed firing through a screen of leaves and twigs without danger to the mortar crew. For the knee-mortar a different method was used, but with the same result. The grenades were time-fused, rather than impact detonated, and this permitted them to be shot through the jungle canopy with the same safety provided by the device used in heavier mortar ammunition. The variable gas chamber of the knee-mortar also gave its handler a scale of ranges which could be lengthened or shortened without varying the angle of the barrel or the early path of the missile.

The assortment of projectiles for the knee-mortar included high explosive shells, grenades, smoke bombs, incendiary shells, signal flares and rockets.

The Japanese 50mm mortar was an extension of the heavy projectile — light weapon concept. With a bore diameter of less than two inches and a weight of 48lb (52lb in the case of the later Type 99 model) this mortar could hurl a 14lb bomb 450 yards or a 7lb missile 2,000 yards — explosive packets all out of proportion to the weapon in calibre and weight. The mortar was, in fact, a spigot projector since the actual projector did not even fit into the barrel of the mortar. (They could not do so because they were some 100mm thick and roughly cubical in shape). The bore was filled and sealed by a long wooden rod, attached to the rear of the projectiles.

Unloaded, the 50mm mortar resembled many conventionally designed European light mortars with an elongated baseplate and a short, light bipod which fitted into the baseplate instead of resting on the ground. The barrel, barrel cap and the socket which fitted into the baseplate was of light construction and the only bulky item of the entire weapon was the baseplate. The traversing mechanism was a crude arrangement, consisting of two arcs cut into the baseplate to permit the bipod legs to be moved and then locked into position by means of wingnuts. There was no elevating mechanism, and the barrel, when the baseplate was level, was set at a fixed angle — 45° to the horizontal.

Range adjustment was obtained by varying the propulsive force, and the 50mm mortar utilised the same variable volume chamber principle as the knee-mortar grenade discharger. A simple gauge was used to adjust the size of the combustion space. By means of a slide clamped to the muzzle it was

Japanese Infantry Weapons

Weapon	Model	Calibre	Length of Piece	MV ft/sec	Weight of Projectile (gr: grains)	Sighted up to (metres)	Rate fire cyclic (rpm)	Type of Feed	Weight in action (lb)
Rifle, Long (1)	Meiji 38 — 1905	6.5mm (.256in)	4ft 3in	2,500	138gr	2,400	—	5rd	8.75
Rifle, Short	Meiji 38 — 1905	6.5mm (.256in)	3ft 2in	—	138gr	2,000	—	magazine	7.5
Rifle, Short (2)	99 — 1939	7.7mm (.303in)	3ft 8in	—	160-200gr	1,500	—	charger loaded	8.8
Grenade discharger	Taisho 10 1921	50mm (1.97in)	1ft 8in	—	18.75oz	250	—	—	5.5
	89 — 1929	50mm (1.97in)	2ft	—	18.75oz / 1.75lb	220 / 700	—	—	10.25
Mortar (3)	98 — 1938	50mm (1.97in)	2ft 1in	—	14lb / 18.5lb	450 / 320	—	—	48
(4)	99 — 1939 small	81mm (3.19in)	2ft 1.25in	—	7lb	2,000	—	—	52
LMG	Taisho 11 1922	6.5mm (.256in)	3ft 7.5in	2,440	138gr	1,500	500	30rd in hopper	22.5
	96 — 1936	6.5mm (.256in)	3ft 6in	2,410	138gr	1,500	550	30rd in mag	20
MMG (2)	99 — 1939	7.7mm (.303in)	3ft 6in	2,300	160-200gr	1,500	800	magazine	22
	Taisho 3 — 1914	6.5mm (.256in)	3ft 9in	—	138gr	2,400	400	strip	67 (127 with tripod)
(2)	92 — 1932	7.7mm (.303in)	3ft 9.5in	2,400	160-200gr	2,700	450	30rd strip	61 (122 with tripod)
AA/anti-tank MG	93 — 1933	13mm (.52in)	7ft 5in	2,250	.114lb	3,600 / 10,800	—	magazine 30rd	7.5cwt
	98 — 1938	20mm (.787in)	4ft 9.5in	2,720	.55lb	5,450 / 12,000 (ceiling)	120	magazine	836 without wheels
Anti-tank rifle	97 — 1937	20mm (.787in)	6ft 10.5in	—	.55lb	1,000	—	magazine	150

possible to control the depth of the missile rod inside the barrel, and the chamber length to a maximum of six inches. Graduations on the slide enabled a wide variation in range with the same propellant charge. By altering the number of propellant increments in the charge it was, of course, possible to make further range adjustments. Propellant increments were supplied as part of the complete round, which also included a lanyard-operated friction primer for insertion in the primer hole in the base of the barrel, and a set of two friction-type pull-igniters for the explosive charge. The strings of these pull-igniters were secured to the mortar after the igniters themselves had been attached to the bomb; when the weapon was fired they would be torn loose, igniting the charge fuse.

At the beginning of the war the standard Japanese medium mortar was the 81mm muzzle-loading Type 97 (M1937) of basic Stokes-Brandt design. Weighing 145lb with a 4ft 1½in long barrel and conventional baseplate, there was little to distinguish it from the medium mortars in service with almost every army in the world. The Type 99 which went into service in 1939 was a modified lightweight and short barrelled version of Type 97. Apart from making drastic reduction in the weight of the barrel and baseplate, a principle was introduced that was not normally utilised in the construction of mortars. The bore was machined so that the ammunition fitted tightly in the bore, so giving improved gas seal.

The barrel of the Type 99 consisted of a straight cylinder 21½in long, and the baseplate was a square ribbed piece of steel with a single socket. A small bipod incorporated elevating, traversing, cross levelling and recoil mechanism; all these mechanisms were contained in the bipod of the larger Type 97 model.

One other exceptional feature in the Type 99 was its firing mechanism. The Type 97 model had a fixed firingpin, but the Type 99 was given a trigger firing mechanism which permitted the bomb to be fired *after* it had seated itself against the breech. This was necessary because the close windage and shorter barrel reduced the impact of the bomb on the firing pin. Firing was effected by striking the head of the firing pin with a wooden mallet or similar instrument.

Notes for table opposite

(1) Also two principal snipers' rifles: Type 91 6.5mm (.256in) and
   Type 99 7.7mm (.303in).
(2) Rimless ammo was provided for the 7.7mm (.303in) rifle, LMG, and MMG, but there was also a semi-rimless ammo which could only be fired by the 92 MMG.
(3) Other mortars included: 1922 model 70mm (2.75in) Type 97 81mm (3.19in), and Type 94 90mm (3.54in).
(4) Sometimes provided with a 14.3lb bomb.
(5) Provided with special AA mountings and sights.

	Model 97	Model 99
Total weight	145lb 2oz	50.8lb
Weight: Tube	45lb 9oz	17.5lb
Weight: Bipod	47lb 12oz	15.0lb
Weight: Baseplate	51lb 12oz	18.3lb
Length of Tube: Interior	45.75in	21.50in
Length of Tube: Overall	45.75in	21.75in
Sights	Collimator	Collimator
Range	3,000yd	2,000yd
Ammunition	HE w/PD fuse	HE w/PD fuse
	(Finned shell)	(Finned shell)

One other heavy mortar was often found with the Japanese infantry. This was the 90mm Type 94 or Type 97 mortar. A muzzle-loading weapon of heavy steel construction, the Type 94 was generally regarded as far too heavy and cumbersome for operations in the jungles of Burma and the South-West Pacific, and it was replaced by the Type 97; the latter was also regarded as too heavy. One distinguishing feature of both these mortars was the two large recoil cylinders mounted on each side of the barrel.

	Type 97	Type 94
Length of barrel, overall	52.375in	50in
Length of barrel, interior	48in	48in
Outside diameter of barrel at muzzle	111mm	103mm
Outside diameter of barrel at base	111mm	116mm
Bore diameter	90mm	90mm
Total weight of mortar	233lb	341.5lb
Weight of barrel	80lb	75lb
Size of base plate	29×18.5in	29×18.5in
Weight of base plate	92lb	89.5lb
Weight of recoil mechanism	None	104lb
Weight of bipod group	61lb	73lb
Recoil (maximum)	6in	
Buffer recoil (maximum)	3.5in	
Type of recoil	Hydro-pneumatic	
Traverse	10 deg	
Weight of bomb	11.5lb	
Dimensions of baseplate	28.5 × 18.5lb	
Range, minimum	610yd	
Range, maximum	4,150yd	

One outstanding feature of both 90mm weapons was their mechanism. The barrel, which fitted into the recoil mechanism was secured by a U-shaped locking pin and supported solely by the ball fitting at base of recoil mechanism. Attached to the top of the bipod were two plungers incorporated indirectly into the buffer system. At the top end of the recoil

Japanese Infantry Support Weapons

Weapon	Model	Calibre	Length of bore (cal)	MV (ft/sec)	Type	Shell Weight (lb)	Range max (yd)	Elevation	Depression	Traverse	Weight in action (lb)	Trail
Anti-tank gun	94 — 1934	37mm (1.45in)	40	2,300	AP HE	1.54	5,500	25°	11°	60°	815	Split
	(1) 1 — 1941	47mm (1.85in)	99.48in	2,700	AP HE	3.37 3.08	—	19°	11°	60°	1,600	Split
Battalion gun	92 gun — 1932	70mm (2.75in)	11	650	HE Shrapnel Smoke	8.36	3,075	50°	10°	45°	468	Split
Regimental gun	Meiji 41 — 1908	75mm (2.95in)	17	1,250	HE Shrapnel AP	14 15	7,800	40°	18°	6°	1,200	Single U
Mountain gun	94 — 1934 mtn gun	75mm (2.95in)	21	1,300	HE Shrapnel Chemical	13.4	9,800	40°	10°	40°	1,200	Split
Field gun	90 — 1930	75mm (2.95in)	44	2,230	HE AP Shrapnel Smoke	14.3	13,300	43°	8°	43°	3,300	Split
Field howitzer	91 — 1931	105mm (4.14in)	24	1,790	HE	35	14,200	45°	7°	56°	4,250	Split
Medium howitzer	Taisho 4 (1915) and later models	150mm (5.90in)	22	1,350	HE, AP CW Shrapnel Smoke	80°	7,560	65°	5°	6°	6,100	Box
	96 (1936)	150mm (5.90in)	22	—	HE, AP Sprapnel Smoke	80°	11,400	75°	7°	30°	8,765	Split

(1) The 47mm (1.85in) anti-tank gun was replaced by the 37mm (1.45in) towards the end of the war.

mechanism were projections which positioned themselves within plungers mounted on the bipod; a screw cover, at lower end of the plungers, covered this junction.

Infantry Guns

Japanese infantry battalions and infantry regiments had their own close support artillery. These guns of 70 and 75mm calibre — correctly referred to as the 'battalion gun' (the 70mm weapon would have been more accurately described as a 'battalion howitzer') and the 'regimental gun' — were the ones which the Japanese deployed in the most forward areas. The 70mm Type 92 (M1932) was the standard battalion equipment, each battalion possessing two; the 75mm Meiji 41 (M1908) was issued on a scale of four to each infantry regiment.

Except perhaps for the 37mm Type 94 anti-tank gun the neat little short-barrelled 70mm battalion howitzer was the most versatile and most mobile of all Japanese light artillery. Easy to handle, it could throw an 8.36lb shell in a high arc to a maximum range of about two miles (3,075yd). The entire weight of the gun and carriage was only 468lb — making it easy to transport into difficult terrain. Wherever the Japanese went their infantry would take the battalion gun. It was designed to be carried by animal transport but when it was broken down into its componets it was man-portable and Japanese infantrymen often lugged this gun up to dominating locations to fire over open sights at Allied positions. Like the 50mm Type 98 mortar, the battalion gun was designed with the heavy projectile-light weapon concept in mind. Because the length of the projectiles was three times as large as the tumbler-sized cartridge case, the ammunition seemed strangely out of proportion.

The most noticeable feature of the 75mm Meiji 41 Regimental gun was the peculiar tubular construction of its single trail. The piece broke down into six pack animal transport loads with a total weight of 1,200lb. Ballistically it was comparable with the American 75mm of World War II. To attain a 7,800yd maximum range the ammunition of the Meiji 41 was necessarily heavier than that of the battalion gun. A higher muzzle velocity — some 1,250ft per second — allowed its shells to keep up with their own sound and strike without warning. This was a marked advantage over the battalion gun, whose slow-moving projectiles (projected at a muzzle velocity of only 650ft per second) proclaimed their arrival long before they landed.

Anti-Tank Guns

Faced with the American threat to the Mariana Islands in May 1944 the Japanese War Office sent reinforcements from Manchuria to the Central Pacific and organised them there in new formations. Infantry battalions in the brigades of these new formations were stronger in heavier weapons than the battalions in standard infantry divisions. In particular the battalion artillery company often had a mountain artillery platoon of three mountain guns, and almost invariably a 'rapid-fire gun' platoon of two anti-tank guns. Mountain guns are discussed in the next chapter, but as anti-tank weapons were primarily manned by infantry it is appropriate to consider them here.

Two anti-tank guns existed: the old Type 94 (M1934) 37mm (1.45in) and the more modern Type I (M1941) 47mm (1.85in). Both were intended as dual purpose weapons, firing solid armour piercing (AP) shot and high explosive shells, and consequently both suffered from the disadvantages inherent in weapons designed for more than one role. The 37mm gun had a muzzle velocity of 2,300ft per second at barrel length of 40in, while the 47mm weapon had a muzzle velocity of 2,700ft per second and barrel length of approximately 100in. Until the invasion of the Philippines the Japanese had rarely had been faced with an armoured threat, and until 1944 the 37mm weapon been primarily employed in a 'battation gun' role. In the event neither the 37mm nor its successor proved to be effective against American-built tanks.

Below: 70mm Type 92 Battalion gun. / *IWM*

Above: Tankette Series M2597. / *IWM*

Right: Tankette Series M2592 (1932). / *IWM*

Chapter 4
Armour

In the Japanese language the word for battle, *sen*, has been combined with the word for wagon, *sha*, to form *sensha*, a tank. Japanese interest in armoured fighting vehicles can be traced back to the 1920s when the British firm of Vickers persuaded the Japanese War Ministry to buy one of the Medium C tanks which Vickers salesmen were endeavouring to sell to a number of foreign powers. In fact the Japanese had already embarked on the building of a heavy tank, but when their designers ran into trouble from lack of experience they decided to adapt foreign designs to their requirements. Thus in 1929 when Japan started producing her own tanks they were based on early models of the French Renault M1917, the Vickers Medium C, and the Carden-Loyd light tank Mark VI. For the most part the Japanese models closely followed the design of the originals. The Type 89A which appeared in 1929, for example, bore a strong resemblance to the original Mark C prototype which Vickers had supplied to Japan in response to their order for a Medium C three years previously. However, the Type 89A had thicker armour, only two machine guns instead of four, and a crew of four instead or the five needed in the Mark C. The Japanese tank also had a stronger suspension, but this and the additional weight of the armour resulted in a slower speed. In effect the Japanese had converted a fast light tank into an infantry support vehicle. The decision to do so was to be reflected in subsequent Japanese armoured policy up to 1945. Tanks were generally regarded as subordinate to the traditional arms, and not as an arm of decision in their own right.

In 1932 the experimental Type 89A was followed by the Type 92, a so-called 'heavy' tank (of 26 tons) whose 34 bogie wheels gave it the appearance of a giant man-made centipede. The Type 92 did not prove successful and the Japanese turned to the design of lighter armoured fighting vehicles more in keeping with their maritime strategy aimed at weaker opponents.

The first Japanese tankette came into service in 1932, and was clearly a development of the Carden Loyd series of weapon carriers. Like the thin-skinned light tank T95 which appeared in quantity three years later, the tankette was used with success against the Chinese in the Sino-Japanese war. The Chinese had no effective equipment with which to counter the Japanese armour and the fact that they frequently conceded a battle when

Japanese tankettes and Type 95s appeared undoubtedly distorted Japanese views of armoured fighting vehicles. While the development of tanks and tank tactics was accelerating in Europe, Japanese technology made little advance, probably because the theatres in which they expected to fight were not suited to uninhibited tank battles. Shortly before the war in Europe, however, Japan did introduce a new tank which owed much to her own designers. This was the medium Type 97, known also as the *Chi-Ha*, which went into service in 1942. Developed from the Type 95, the *Chi-Ha* was eventually developed to carry a variety of armaments, including in one version a 150mm gun, and in another, a 300mm mortar.

By European standards the armour of the Japanese tanks was thin, but the main armament was comparable with equivalent British and American tanks so far as calibre and weight of projectile was concerned.

General Characteristics
Classification: Japanese tanks were divided into:

Tankettes	:	3 to 4.5 tons
Light Tanks	:	up to 10 tons
Medium	:	10 to 20 tons
Heavy	:	over 20 tons

Tanks were named after the manufacturer, and — like their other weapons and military stores — numbered by the Japanese calendar year, dates being taken from 660 BC (which was their year 00). Thus the European equivalent of a year date is found by subtracting 660.

Turrets: were all round or oval.
Armament: In some models a machine gun was mounted in the back plate of the turret. Special machine gun compartments were often built out of the superstructure. Machine guns were seldom, if ever, mounted coaxially with the main armament.
Armour: The most heavily armoured Japanese tank of World War II was the obsolescent M2595, 27ton heavy tank, with 35mm (1.38in) armour on the front.

This was inadequate in a tank of this weight. The Japanese generally used rolled armour with welded and riveted joints, both types of joint being commonly found in the same tank. The use of curved plates was a common feature.
Suspension: In the tankette, and the latest light and medium tanks, the Japanese used modified Carden-Loyd suspension in which the weight of the tank was supported by horizontal compression springs arranged inside tubular protective casings on each side of the hull between the bogie wheels and return rollers.
Speed: Maximum speeds were not high, but the power-weight ratios (25 for the light tank) resulted in good cross-country speeds.
Lightness: The Japanese have emphasised lightness, and track pressures were low, giving an important advantage when travelling over soft ground.

Above: Tankette Series 2597 being winched away by a Japanese light tractor. / *IWM*

Centre left: Tankette Type M2592. / *IWM*

Bottom left: Tankette Series M2592. / *IWM*

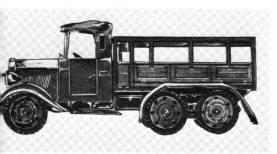

Top left: Naval armoured car Type 2592.

Top right: Early model of light tank (M2593).

Centre left: Medium tank early model (M2594).

Centre right: Light tank M2595.

Above left: Army truck Type 94A.

Above right: Tractor Type 92A.

Left: Sumida armoured car-trolley.

Left: Tankette Series M2592. / *IWM*

Below: Light tank Series 2592 supporting an internal security operation in China in the early 1930s. / *IWM*

Bottom: Light tank Series M2595 crossing a river in Hunan in 1941. / *IWM*

Insulation: Woven asbestos heat insulation was placed inside the hull and turret of the tankette and light tank.

Engines: The Japanese used air-cooled diesel engines.

Accommodation: By European standards crew accommodation was cramped.

Characteristics of Individual AFVs
Japanese Tankette: Series M2592, M2594
Length: 11ft Width: 5ft 3in Height 5ft 4in
Weight: 3 tons Speed: 20-25mph
Armament: One machine gun in turret
Armour: Front: 14mm (.55in) Sides: 8mm (.31in) Turret: 14mm (.55in)
Crew: Two

The engine of the tankette was on left side and to the front. The turret was mounted on rear of hull superstructure, giving a general boot-shape impression. The round turret contained a machine gun in a ball mounting; the glacis plate was long and sloping; there were four bogie wheels in two pans.

Light Tank: Early Model, series M2593
Length: 14ft 8in Width: 5ft 10in Height: 6ft
Weight: 7 tons Speed: 28mph
Armament: One light machine gun in turret. One light machine gun in front superstructure
Armour: Up to 22mm (.87in)
Crew: Three

This model had a small, high and round turret with sloping sides, and its machine guns were in ball mountings. There were three bogies each with two small wheels and semi-elliptic springing.

Light Tank: Series M2595
Length: 14ft 4in Width: 6ft 9in Height: 7ft
Weight: Unladen 7 tons, in action 8-9 tons Speed: 28mph
Armament: One 37mm (1.45in) gun in turret. One machine gun in rear of turret. One machine gun in superstructure
Armour: Front: 12mm (.47in) Sides: 10-12mm (.39-.47in) Turret: 12mm (.47in)
Crew: Four

This tank was distinguished by a rounded turret with square front on medium high superstructure. The sides of the superstructure protruded over top of tracks, and there were four bogie wheels in two pairs on each side.

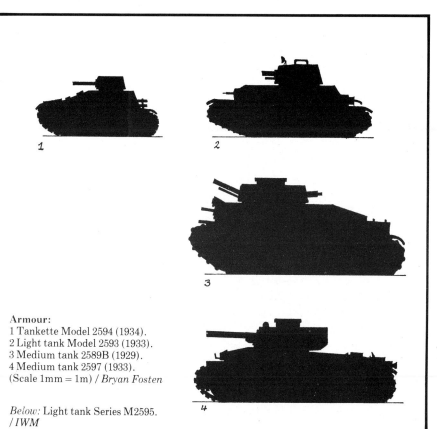

Armour:
1 Tankette Model 2594 (1934).
2 Light tank Model 2593 (1933).
3 Medium tank 2589B (1929).
4 Medium tank 2597 (1933).
(Scale 1mm = 1m) / *Bryan Fosten*

Below: Light tank Series M2595.
/ *IWM*

Medium Tank: Early Model, series M2594
(This tank, based on the old Vickers Mark C, was considered obsolescent in 1941)
Length: 20ft 10in Width: 8ft 4in Height: 8ft 6in
Weight: 14 tons Speed: 28mph
Armament: One 37mm (1.45in) in turret. One light machine gun in rear of turret. One light machine gun in front hull
Armour: Front and turret: 17mm (.67in) Sides: 11mm (.43in)
Crew: Five

This model had a rounded turret, sloping sides, and a machine gun ball-mounted in rear of the turret. Its superstructure protruded over tops of nine small bogie wheels which were almost entirely obscured by skirting. The rear of hull was fitted with a tail to increase trench-crossing performance.

Medium Tank: Series M2595 and M2597
Length: 18ft Width: 7ft 8in Height: 7ft 2.5in
Weight: Unladen 13ton 6cwt, in action 15 tons Speed: 25mph max
Armament: One 57mm (2.24in) gun in turret. One machine gun in rear of turret. One machine gun in front superstructure
Armour: Front: 25mm (.98in) Sides: 15mm (.59in)
Crew: Four

This series was recognised by the rounded turret with a machine gun in a ball mounting facing rear. A second machine gun was housed in a superstructure to the left. There were six medium-sized bogie wheels and a hand-rail type aerial around the top of the turret.

Heavy Tanks
The so-called heavy tank, series M2595, did not see action in World War II — being considered obsolete. With a length of 21ft, width 8.5ft and height of 9.5ft, this vehicle weighed 27 tons and was said to have a maximum speed of 13.5mph. As armament it carried one 70mm (2.76in) gun, one 37mm (1.45in) gun and two machine guns.

An obsolete 38 ton Japanese imitation of the Vickers Independent 1925/26, known as the Ishi 108 was also said to exist at the beginning of the war.

Armoured Cars
Armoured cars are usually regarded as reconnaissance or liaison vehicles, whose prime mission is to gain information or liaise between various units. They are intended to fight only as a last resort and for this they need to be highly mobile. The Japanese Sumida M2593 fitted this specification. It had few refinements but it could be re-wheeled to run on the railway tracks which often provided a better alternative to the roads in the Far East. Known as an armoured car-trolley because in 20 minutes it could be converted into an armoured trolley to run on the railway lines, the Sumida was extensively used in Manchuria for the protection of railway battalions from

Above: Light tanks
crossing flooded fields
near Tokyo in 1941.
/ *IWM*

Centre left: Light tank
Series M2595 / *IWM*

Bottom left: Light tank
Series M2595. / *IWM*

guerillas and bandits. In this role light armoured wagons were sometimes coupled to it to form a light armoured train for a rapid advance or to move small groups of troops quickly. The Sumida armoured car's characteristics were as follows:

Length: 15ft 9in Width: 5ft 11in Height: 7ft 7in
Weight: 6.5 tons Speed: 50mph
Armament: One heavy machine gun in turret. Seven rifle slits
Armour: Up to 16mm (.63in)
Crew: Four-six

The Sumida was the standard Army armoured car, but two other types existed. The Japanese Naval six-wheeled armoured car was often landed with detachments of the Imperial Navy destined for garrison duties. Characteristics were as follows:

Length: 15ft 8in Width: 5ft 10in Height: 7ft 6in
Weight: 6.5 tons Speed: 50mph
Armament: Four light machine guns
Armour: 8-11mm (.31-.43in)
Crew: Four-six

The other type, the Osaka, also a six-wheeled vehicle, was an improvisation built on a commercial long chassis, and distinguished by twin tyres on the rear wheels. Its characteristics were as follows:

Length: 16ft 4in Width: 6ft 1in Height: 8ft 8in
Weight: 5.8 tons Speed: 37mph
Armament: Two light machine guns
Armour: 8-11mm (.31-.43in)
Crew: Four-five

Armoured Trains
In Manchuria the Japanese used armoured trains, consisting principally of tank-like armoured freight cars, each mounting four machine guns and equipped to carry 18 riflemen apiece. With an armoured engine as the propulsion unit, such trains were made up of combinations of armoured freight cars, with a box-car for headquarters, trucks carrying 75mm field guns, machine gun trucks and trucks with sleepers, rails and materials to repair damaged railway lines.

Miscellaneous Armour
Amphibious Tanks
In China, in 1939, the Japanese used amphibious tanks to cross a river near Changsa. These tanks were a variation of their early model of light tank, and similar to the Vickers amphibious, relying on a collapsible screen and not a bulky pontoon, to keep them afloat. These tanks did not appear again,

Above: Armoured railway car used in Manchuria.

Left: Light tank Series M2595. / *IWM*

Above left: Medium tank, early model Series M2594. / *IWM*

Centre left: Medium tank Type 2597. / *IWM*

Bottom left: Medium tank, early model Series M2594. / *IWM*

Above: Medium tank Series 2597. / *IWM*

Right: Medium tanks Series M1594 (early models). / *IWM*

but T95s were floated across Pacific island rivers by means of pontoon devices carried by Japanese engineer units.

Tank Trailers
Ammunition and stores were carried in trailers towed either by tankettes or light tanks. Up to 3,300lb could be transported in such trailers, the most advanced of which were tracked with a pair of bogie wheels each side and a rocker arm suspension.

Support Vehicles
Work tanks for company supply sections had the same chassis as the medium tank, with a box body taking the place of the turret. Crane tanks were a variation of the work tanks, being fitted with a motor-driven crane at the rear.

Ammunition and Vulnerability
The shell for the 94 type 37mm (1.45in) tank gun was supplied in boxes of 10 rounds, weighing 37lb. The 90 type 57mm (2.24in) tank gun fired either an armour-piercing shell of an HE of the same weight. Both were packed in boxes of 10 rounds, weighing 88lb.

Medium tanks carried 20 rounds per gun, and 2,000-3,000 rounds of machine gun ammunition.

British and American small arms ammunition penetrated the Japanese tankette and light tank. Vickers .51in (12.8mm) AP could penetrate the sides and put out of action the tracks of medium and light tanks, and the British .55in armour-piercing bullet fired from the 'Boys' anti-tank rifle would undoubtedly penetrate the front, but there is no record of it doing so.

However 47mm (1.85in), 37mm (1.45in) and 20mm (.79in) anti-tank guns firing AP certainly proved effective against the 94 type medium tank at 880 yards.

Armoured Tactics
It is rarely possible to assess the capabilities of a weapon unless it is considered in relation to its tactical employment. A brief summary of the Japanese attitude towards the use of armour and their experience is therefore desirable.

Being obsessed with the value of the attack it was to be expected that Japanese training of tank troops stressed the offensive. Two main battle doctrines were taught — the attack and the pursuit; little consideration was given to the defence. The attack was supposed to be carried out with speed and deception, the basic principle being to 'anchor' the enemy by frontal action while enveloping him from flanks and rear. Little thought seem to have been given to the independent use of armour, and Japanese Field Service Manuals emphasised the use of *all* arms at each successive stage of a battle. Tanks and armoured cars could be used in a variety of ways; if enough were available and the circumstances were right they could even be used on independent raids. But their main role was to assist and protect infantry.

Above: Medium tank Type 2594 supporting an infantry action in China in 1940. Notice that the infantryman in the middle foreground carries his bayonet fixed. / *IWM*

Left: Medium tank Type M2594. / *IWM*

77

Above left: Medium tank Type M2594. /*IWM*

Left: Medium tank Type 2597. /*IWM*

Top: Medium tank Type 2589 (early model). /*IWM*

Above: Heavy tanks (early model). /*IWM*

Right: Japanese mobile workshop. /*IWM*

Japanese Terms Used in Connection with Armour

Tank	*sensha*
Tank corps	*senshatai*
Tankette	*keisokosha*
Light tank	*kei sensha*
Medium tank	*chu sensha*
Heavy tank	*ju sensha*
Supply tank	*hokyu sensha*
Battle tank	*sento sensha*
Bridging tank	*gakyo sensha*
Ammunition tank	*danyaku yusoyo sensha*
Armoured car	*soko jidosha*
Armoured train	*soko ressha*
Tank commander	*sensha cho*
Tank officer	*sensha shoko*
Tank crew	*sensha jion*
Tank engineers	*senshatai-zuki kohei*
Tank section	*sensha shotai*
Tank company	*sensha chutai*
Tank battalion	*sensha daitai*
Tank brigade	*sensha ryodan*
Tank regiment	*sensha rentai*
Divisional tank company	*shidan sensha chutai*
Tank bridging company	*gakyo sensha chutai*
Tank brigade MT company	*sensha ryodan yuso chutai*
Tank pool	*sensha sho*
Tank attack	*sensha no kogeki*
Tank (route) reconnaissance	*sensha (shinro no) teisatsu*
Tank mine	*tai-sensha jirai*
Tank obstacle	
Tank trap	*sensha shogaibutsua*

And this was invariably the way they were used. Tanks preceded Japanese infantry on occasions; they moved off with infantry from a given start line, and they often followed. They were used as reserve, as pursuit troops, against the garrisons of walled towns and against guerillas in open fields. But rarely were they employed in the way that armoured forces were used in the West. In the final drive on Hankow in 1938 a new formation of mechanised artillery and motorised infantry was formed in the field, but as soon as its mission was accomplished, this embryo armoured division was disbanded.

In November 1937 three Japanese tanks formed a stationary battery while infantry were crossing the Suchow Canal, and in February 1938, 40 tanks were similarly employed at the crossing of the River Hwai. A few months later, tanks were used as pursuit troops — driving along both sides of the Yangtze at the same time.

In 1938, during the attack on Suchowfu, tanks made a wide circling dash and cut the railway lines nearly 40 miles from the city. Four years later, in the battle of Kuala Dipang (Malaya) having failed in encircling attacks, the Japanese brought tanks into action straight down the road. On this occasion men of the Argyll and Sutherland Highlanders 'hid in the jungle, joined with units of a Punjab regiment and successfully attacked the follow-up Japanese infantry, inflicting on them losses of seven or eight to one'.

At the battle of Slim River, Malaya 1942, in the same year, the Japanese were once again foiled in their encircling move. They again attacked with tanks — 30 of them moving straight down the road to a depth of 20 miles.

At Milne Bay a few light tanks were used and about ten on Guadalcanal. On each occasion their use was restricted by the terrain, but on neither was there any outstanding tactical employment.

The one factor steadily apparent in Japanese armoured tactics was that of constant change to meet conditions as they occurred. Tankettes were originally planned for bringing up ammunition in their tracked trailers to the front lines; for the evacuation of casualties; and for reconnaissance in the manner of an armoured weapons carrier such as the Bren. But tankettes came to be seen as tanks, and nearly all Japanese landings in China were made with a force of two divisions, each disembarked with a tankette unit.

Tankettes were usually landed from the square stern of landing boats beached stern first, baulks of timber being used to extend the landing platform. At the landing near Do Son the Japanese put ashore 2,000 troops, three medium tanks, artillery and 10 tankettes in 20 minutes.

In assault on walled towns tanks played a decisive role, but not by battering the ramparts. The attacking force was divided into four columns — one column attacking the front wall, while two other columns attacked the adjacent sides; the rear was purposely left free from attack. Artillery blew breaches in the two near corners; and then infantry entered and moved through the town, driving the enemy from the rear. Meantime the fourth column of tanks waited until the enemy were well into the open and then, from ambush or by a wide encircling movement, cut them down.

Above left: Sumida armoured car-trolley. /*IWM*

Centre left: Armoured recovery vehicle. /*IWM*

Bottom left: Naval 6-wheeled armoured car. /*IWM*

Above: Amphibian tank Type 2 KA-ML. /*IWM*

Centre right: Rear view of amphibious tank showing detachable pontoon. /*IWM*

Bottom right: Amphibious tank (fitted with pontoons). See previous photograph for rear view. /*IWM*

Japanese Armoured Cars

Type	Weight (tons)	Crew	Armour	Armament	Dimensions	Engine	Speed	Suspension	Remarks
Sumida 6-wheel (armoured car trolley)	6.5	4-6	Up to 16mm (.63in)	1 HMG in turret 7 rifle slits	Length 15ft 9in Width 5ft 11in Height 7ft 7in	40hp petrol	50mph	6 wheels	Carried 6 rims for use on railway line Round cupola on van-shaped body
Osaka 6-wheel (armoured car)	5-8	4-5	8-11mm (.31-.43in)	2 LMGs	Length 16ft 4in Width 6ft 1in Height 8ft 8in	35hp petrol 4-cylinder water cooled	37mph	6 wheels	Commercial lorry chassis Twin tyres on rear wheels
Naval 6-wheel (armoured car)	6.5	4-6	8-11mm (.31-.43in)	4 LMGs	Length 15ft 8in Width 5ft 10in Height 7ft 6in	85hp 6-cylinder water cooled	50mph	6 wheels	Used by naval landing parties Belly clearance 1ft 4in

Japanese Tanks

Type	Weight (tons)	Crew	Armour	Armament	Dimensions	Engine	Drive	Speed	Suspension
Tankette (Series M2592, 2594, etc)	3	2	Turret 14mm (.55in) Hull front 14mm Hull sides 8mm (.31in)	One MG in ball mounting in turret	Length 11ft Width 5ft 3in Height 5ft 4in	Petrol 45-50hp 4-cylinder air-cooled	Front sprocket	20-25mph (max)	4 bogie wheels each side in pairs

Type	Weight (tons)	Crew	Armour	Armament	Dimensions	Engine	Drive/Speed	Suspension
Light Tank (Early Model, M2593)	7	3	Up to 22mm (.87in)	One LMG in front turret One LMG in front superstructure	Length 14ft 8in Width 5ft 10in Height 6ft	Petrol 85hp 6-cylinder air-cooled	Front sprocket 28mph (max)	6 small bogie wheels each side, in pairs
Light Tank (Series M2595, etc)	Unladen 7 In action 8-9	4	Turret 12mm (.47in) Hull front 12mm Hull sides 10-12mm (.40-.47in) Hull rear 12mm	One 37mm (1.45in) gun in front turret One MG right rear of turret One MG in left front superstructure	Length 14ft 4in Width 6ft 9in Height 7ft	Diesel 240hp at 2,000rpm air-cooled	Front sprocket 28mph at 2,000rpm	4 bogie wheels each side, in pairs
Medium Tank (Early Model, M2594)	14	4	Front 17mm (.67in) Sides 11mm (.43in) Turret 17mm	One 37mm (1.45in) gun in front turret One MG in rear of turret One MG in front superstructure	Length with tail 20ft 10in Width 8ft 4in Height 8ft 6in	Petrol 160hp 6-cylinder air-cooled	Front sprocket 28mph (max)	9 small bogie wheels and protective skirting
Medium Tank (Series M2595 2597, etc)	Unladen 13.5 In action 15	4	Front 25mm (.98in) Sides 15mm (.59in) Top 8mm (.31in)	One 57mm (2.24in) gun in front turret One MG in rear turret One MG in front superstructure	Length 18ft Width 7ft 8in Height 7ft 2.5in	Diesel 12-cylinder air cooled	Front sprocket 25mph (max)	6 medium sized bogie wheels each side
Heavy Tank (Early Model, M2595)	27	5	Up to 35mm (1.38in)	One 70mm (2.75in) gun One 37mm (1.45in) gun and two MGs	Length 21ft 3in Width 8ft 10in Height 9ft 6in	290hp	Front sprocket 13.5mph	6 small bogie wheels each side in pairs

Above: 75mm (2.95in) Meiji 41 (1908) Regiment gun disassembled into pack loads. / *IWM*

Below: 75mm field gun M95. / *IWM*

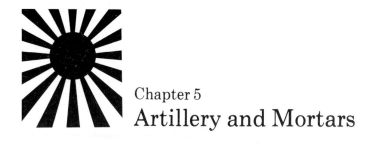

Chapter 5
Artillery and Mortars

Field Artillery

Japanese 70mm and 75mm Regimental guns were described in Chapter 3. Apart from these weapons, which were organic to all infantry battalions, field artillery support was provided by the field artillery regiment in a standard infantry division or by an artillery battalion attached to the independent infantry brigades. Field artillery and mountain regiments were both similarly organised into three battalions each equipped with 12 75mm (2.95in) guns. These guns were copies or developments of an early Krupp design — the latest Type 95 (M1935) field piece capable of hurling a 14.3lb HE, AP, shrapnel or smoke shell to a maximum range of 12,000yd. This particular gun had an all-up weight in action of slightly less than 2,500lb, while its 1930 predecessor weighed 800lb more but could hurl the same projectile 13,300yd. The mountain gun fired a 13.4lb shell and had a range of 9,800yd.

Independent mountain artillery regiments differed from their divisional counterparts in having two battalions instead of three. Each battalion had three companies and battalion transport (which was additional to regimental transport). Regimental strength was approximately 2,500 all ranks; armament, 24 guns — normally the 75mm (2.95in) mountain guns. One regiment operating in the SW Pacific had a strength of about 1,500. But it had left a large part of its transport in rear areas, and had only three guns to the company instead of the normal four, a pioneer section taking the place of the fourth gun section.

Medium Artillery

105mm 'field howitzers', classed by the Japanese as 'heavy' artillery, were issued to three of the old *Ko* (Type A) divisions. These guns, which first appeared in 1931, were constructed to a design based on a 1905 Schneider howitzer. With an all-up weight in action of nearly two tons they were cumbersome cannons. But they could throw a 35lb shell a distance of 11,500yd.

Medium artillery, as such, were equipped either with 105mm guns, or 150mm Taisho 4 or Type 96 (M1936) howitzers. There were in fact two models of 105mm guns — the Type 14, issued in 1925, and the Type 92, which went into service in 1932; both were towed by tractors. By 1939 the

Above: 105mm Howitzer M91. *IWM*   *Below:* 105mm Howitzer M91 (1931). / *IWM*

Above: 150mm medium Howitzer M96
(1936). / *IWM*

Below: 150mm medium Howitzer M96
(1936). / *IWM*

Type 14 was considered to be obsolete, and the 1932 weapon — weighing about three tons in action, and firing a 33lb HE projectile to a range of 20,000yd — predominated.

Of the medium howitzers the Taisho 4 and a number of improved models of it, together with the Type 96 saw considerable action against Allied forces. The Taisho 4, weighing nearly three tons in action could shoot an 80lb projectile 7,500yd, while the modern Type 96 — weighing a ton more than its predecessor — could better this range by a further 3,800yd. Medium howitzer regiments carried a total of 2,760 rounds of HE in their first and second line transport; medium gun regiments carried 2,592 rounds.

'Field Heavy' Artillery

150mm Type 89 guns and 240mm Type 45 howitzers are considered in this category because they had a certain degree of mobility. The Type 89 gun, for example, was tractor-drawn, while the old (1912) Type 45 240mm howitzers were broken down and transported in 10 vehicles to each weapon. The 150mm gun which weighed about 7.5 tons in action could fire an 80lb shell 10 miles (22,000yd). The old 240mm howitzer had only half this range — 11,000yd — but its projectile weighed 400lb.

Heavy and Fortress Weapons

These weapons are detailed in the accompanying table. Apart from a 24mm railway gun there were several low trajectory and high angle siege pieces which were principally deployed as fortress armament. Prime movers for the 410mm howitzers and 240mm railway gun were of prewar American manufacture.

Anti-Aircraft Artillery

Standard Japanese anti-aircraft weapons ran the gamut of calibres from that of the 7.7mm (.303in) medium machine gun to 105mm heavy guns. In addition to the Army's own weapons a number of naval pieces were also pressed into service — especially towards the end of the war.

In the smaller calibres the 13.2mm Hotchkiss dual purpose heavy machine gun — which fired its little .52in projectiles at a muzzle velocity of 2,250ft per second, to a vertical height of 13,000ft — acquired a good reputation in China. The 20mm quick-firing gun of the Japanese machine cannon units which boosted its half-pound shell, by nearly 500ft per second more was also well thought of. This was an Oerlikon type weapon. Both guns were light, fairly mobile and fitted with flash eliminators to reduce the chance of enemy aircraft spotting their location. 25mm naval pom-poms and old (1931 vintage) 40mm Vickers type naval machine cannons were also employed. But the Army's stand-bys for defence against air attack were 75s of two models. One was introduced in 1922 and the other in 1928. The older gun had a velocity of only 1,800ft per second and would not reach as far into the skies as the later version, which had 560ft per second more muzzle velocity. But guns handled 14½lb explosive shells. The practical rate of fire was 10-12 rounds per minute with the older gun and 20 rounds with the 1928

Above: 75mm anti-aircraft gun M88. / *IWM*   *Below:* 25mm AA gun M96 (1936). / *IWM*

Above: 13.2mm
AA/Atk gun M93
(1935) on a drive
mounting. / IWM

Centre left: 75mm AA
gun M88 in travelling
position. / IWM

Bottom left: AA range
finder with 2-metre
base. / IWM

Top right: 3in Naval
gun installed for AA
and coast defence.
/ IWM

Bottom right: 3in
Naval gun installed for
AA and coast defence.
/ IWM

Above: 37mm anti-tank gun M94. / *IWM*   *Below:* 47mm anti-tank gun MI (1941). /*IWM*

weapon; although a rate of 25rpm was claimed for both. Vertical ranges were around 20,000ft for the 1922 gun, and 30,000ft for the later model; 11,000yd and 15,000yd respectively were claimed as horizontal ranges.

Some AA battalions deployed primarily in the defence of the home islands were equipped with 105mm guns. Of 1925 vintage these guns projected 35lb missiles at a muzzle velocity of 2,300ft per second. Vertical range was around 36,000ft and the horizontal was about 21,999ft; rate of fire was eight rounds per minute.

Other AA guns worthy of mention and included in the table of AA weapons are the obsolescent pedestal mounted 76.2mm (3in) naval AA gun and the 1929 model 127mm (5in) heavy naval gun.

Anti-Tank Artillery

Most of the Japanese anti-tank weapons were with the infantry, and the infantrymen were trained to deal with tanks with grenades and close assault weapons. This meant moving in on enemy armour and personal assaults with anti-tank mines, explosive and incendiary (Molotov cocktail) charges.

Artillery weapons which were considered suitable for use in an anti-tank role were the infantry 75mm Regimental gun (of which each infantry regiment had four), the 70mm Battalion gun — of which there were two in each infantry battalion; together with the 75mm Mountain guns and the 75mm field guns of the field artillery regiments. Armour piercing ammunition was issued for use with all these weapons.

Independent anti-tank units were equipped either with the 37mm (1.45in) or the 47mm (1.85in) anti-tank gun. With a muzzle velocity of 2,300ft per second the 37mm weapon's 1.5lb solid shot was said to be capable of piercing one inch of armour at normal; the more modern 47mm gun with a muzzle velocity of 2,700ft per second could double this performance. Both weapons had a lateral traverse of 60° on their split trails, and a vertical elevation from −11° to +25° in the case of the 37mm and −11° to +19° with the 47mm gun.

Until the invasion of the Philippines it must be remembered that the Japanese had had virtually no anti-tank problem to worry about and the 37mm gun was relatively untried.

Mortar Units

The standard 81mm mortars have been described in Chapter 3. These *Hakugeki* weapons were in fact sometimes issued to Japanese artillery units.

The so-called 'medium' mortars issued to mortar battalions were in fact 15cm weapons. Heavy and ungainly in appearance they were of conventional design — smooth-bore, muzzle-loaded, bipod mounted — little more, in fact, than enlarged versions of the 81mm weapon.

Weighing 778lb, the 15cm Model 97 fired an HE bomb of 56lb to a maximum range of 2,300yd. Bursting radius of the bomb was said to be 65ft.

The weapon was assembled and operated like any other Stokes-Brandt mortar; its only peculiarly Japanese characteristic was a firing mechanism like that of the 81mm Model 99 weapon, which used a firing pin camshaft built into the base cap instead of a fixed firing pin.

Independent artillery mortar battalions (*Dokunitsu Kyoho Daitai*) in Burma were issued with a ponderous 250mm Type 98 (M1938) spigot mortar which could throw a 700lb bomb about 1,000yd. This weapon was clearly akin to the 320mm spigot mortar designed specifically for demolition work. (Few of them were made and they were little used).

In both cases the spigot mortar itself comprised a steel spigot, a domed steel mounting plate — supported by a dome-shaped wooden block, and a steel baseplate; these were all bolted to a heavy wood block base. The spigot was a steel cylinder with a cavity at the upper end for the propellant. The wooden base consisted of three sections of rectangular baulks of timber, the top section, the middle and the bottom sections — alternate sections being laid at rightangles to one another.

Provision was made for a limited amount of traverse and the spigot-seating bolts were so constructed as to permit setting up for line. Changes in range were obtained by varying the propellant charge.

Bombs were in three parts which screwed together; an HE warhead fitted with a nose-fuse, a cylindrical central portion with an internal cavity for a secondary filling, and a cylindrical finned tail unit.

The primary and augmenting charges were contained in a brass case which fitted into the spigot cavity; ignition was by means of an electric ignitor through a flash channel in the side of the spigot and the bomb tail.

Two other artillery weapons also deserve mention: the 70mm Taisho, Model 2 (1922) and the 70mm 'Barrage' or 'Spike' mortar.

The Taisho 2, a clumsy muzzle-loaded and rifled weapon, was declared obsolescent early in the war. Its significant feature was its wooden base-plate which mounted the whole weapon, and the fact that it had no bipod — an elevating screw being attached to the baseplate. This mortar necessarily had a slow rate of fire because of the time taken by the projectile to seat itself in the barrel before firing. The 70mm 'Barrage' mortar was in effect a very simple, muzzle-loading smooth bore weapon, firing a projectile which ejected a number of small parachute-suspended explosive tubes. It was effective against low flying aircraft if used in sufficient numbers, as a small number of these mortars could maintain a dangerous 'barrage' of floating bomb tubes in the air.

The barrel was mounted on a wooden baseplate with a spike on its lower side — the spike being an iron rod about one inch thick and 18in long. Laying the mortar was determined solely by the angle at which the rod was stuck into the ground, and there was no way of traversing or elevating it. Nor was there any method of fire control.

The round was fired by dropping it into the mortar in the usual fashion. Ignition of the propelling charge ignited a delay element in the projectile, which, in due course, ignited an expelling charge in the projectile. This expelling charge expelled seven canisters from the projectile, the seven canisters and two sections of the projectile case being carried away on small

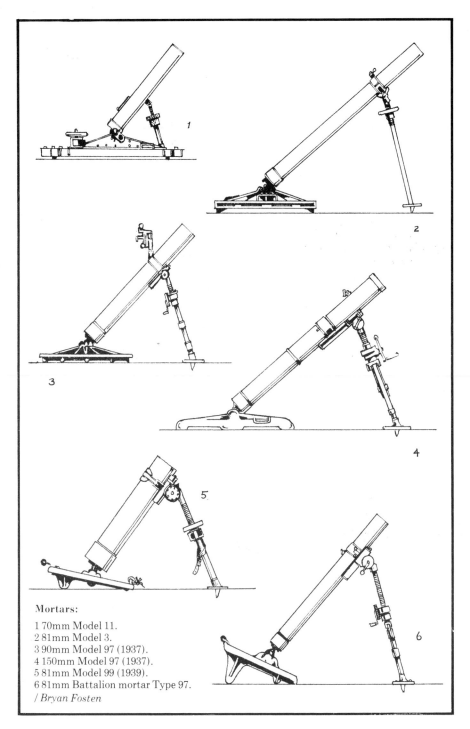

Mortars:

1 70mm Model 11.
2 81mm Model 3.
3 90mm Model 97 (1937).
4 150mm Model 97 (1937).
5 81mm Model 99 (1939).
6 81mm Battalion mortar Type 97.
/ *Bryan Fosten*

(1) The Japanese also used a Model 92 (1932) 7.7mm (.303in) MG almost identical with the Lewis, which fired British .303in, MkVII ammunition.

(2) The Japanese also used a 20mm (.79in) AA, MG, Oerlikon model.

---

parachutes. The canisters in turn ejected high explosive 'shrapnel' tubes, which detonated violently. Each of the seven shrapnel tubes was 3½in long by 11/16in in diameter, and each contained a little less than ½oz of explosive.

This mortar had an effective vertical range of 3,000-4,000ft. However, as there was no way of adjusting the time delay of the projectile, the altitude of burst depended largely on the angle of elevation at which the mortar was fired. The shrapnel tubes were the only components containing high explosive, and the major hazard was the blast effects of these tubes — approximately 10yd; the fragments produced by the explosion were too small to be effective.

Below: 70mm barrage mortar. / *IWM*

Japanese AA Weapons (including Dual Purpose and Naval)

Model	Calibre	Range, max (a) Vertical (ft) (b) Horizontal (yd)	Rate of fire practical	Weight in action	MV (ft/sec)	Ammunition	Weight of projectile	Remarks
92 (1932)	7.7mm (.303in)	(a) 4,000 (est) (b) 4,600	300-350	122lb	2,400	Ball, AP Incendiary, tracer	0.47oz	The infantry MG fitted with AA adaptor Hotchkiss type (1) and special AA sights
93 (1933)	13.2mm (.52in)	(a) 13,000 (b) 7,000 (Ground sight to 3,600 metres)	250-300	7.5cwt (double) Gun alone 87lb	2,250	Ball, AP, tracer	.114lb	Single (pedestal) mount Douple (tripod) mount 30rd magazine
98 (1938)	20mm (.79in)	(a) 12,000 (b) 5,450	120-150	836lb without wheels	2,720	HE, AP, tracer, HR tracer (SD)	.55lb	Dual purpose AA/Atk weapon, carried by machine cannon units (2)
96 (1936)	25mm (.98in)	(a) 14,000 (b) 5,700	175-200	5,330lb (triple mount) Single gun only 246lb	2,978	HE, AP, HE tracer (SD), HE white phosphorous	.55lb	Single mount Twin (pedestal mount) 15rd magazine
91 (1931)	40mm (1.57in)	(a) 13,000 (b) 5,000	60-100 per barrel	1,960lb single 3,130lb twin	2,000	Tracer, AP, HE HE with time fuse	1.52lb	Vickers type, single and double (pedestal) mounts
11 (1922) 35 cal	75mm (2.95in)	(a) 19,600 (b) 11,000	10-12	4,800lb	1,800	HE	14.5lb	Obsolescent
88 (1928) 40 cal	75mm (2.95in)	(a) 30,000 (b) 15,000	20	5,390lb	2,360	HE Incendiary Shrapnel	14.6lb	Principal Army AA gun
10 (1921) 40 cal	76.2mm (3in)	(a) 25,000 (b) 12,000	15		2,220	HE Incendiary Shrapnel	12.7lb	Pedestal mount
14 (1925)	105mm (4.14in)	(a) 36,000 (b) 20,000	8	7 tons	2,300	HE	35lb	Navy AA gun
89 (1929)	127mm (5in)	(a) 35,000 (b) 15,000	8-10		2,370	HE, AP, fixed and semi-fixed	50lb	Single (pedestal) and double mount

Japanese Artillery Anti-tank, Mountain and Field

Weapon	Model	Calibre	Length of bore (cal)	MV (ft/sec)	Type	Shell Weight (lb)	Range max (yd)	Elevation	Depression	Traverse	Weight in action (lb)	Trail	Remarks
Anti-tank gun	94 — 1934	37mm (1.45in)	40	2,300	AP, HE	1.54	5,500	25°	11°	60°	815	Split	—
Anti-tank gun	11 — 1041	47mm (1.85in)	99.48	2,700	AP, HE	3.37 3.08	—	19°	11°	60°	1,600	Split	Pneumatic tyres Adapted for towing by MT
Mountain mtn gun	94 — 1934	75mm (2.95in)	21	1,300	HE, Shrapnel, Chemical AP	13.4	9,800	40°	10°	40°	1,200	Split	Also hollow charge ammo
Field gun	38 — 1905	75mm (2.95in)	—	—	HE, AP, Shrapnel, Smoke	14.3	9,025	16°	8°	7°	2,083	Box	Obsolescent in 1938
Field gun	38 — 1905 improved	75mm	108in (barrel)	—	HE, AP, Shrapnel, Smoke	14.3	12,565	43°	8°	7°	2,448	Open box	
Field gun	90 — 1930	75mm	44	2,230	HE, AP, Shrapnel, Smoke	14.3	13,300	43°	8°	43°	3,300	Split	Prominent muzzle collar
Field gun	95 — 1935	75mm	—	1,640	HE, AP, Shrapnel, Smoke, Chemical	14.3	12,000	43°	8°	50°	2,438	Split	
Field howitzer	91 — 1931	105mm (4.14in)	24	1,790	HE, AP Shrapnel Chemical	35	11,500	45°	7°	45°	4,250	Split	Also hollow charge ammo

Japanese Artillery Medium, Field Heavy and Siege

Weapon	Model	Calibre	Length of bore (cal)	MV (ft/sec)	Type	Shell Weight (lb)	Range max (yd)	Elevation	Depression	Traverse	Weight in Action (lb)	Trail	Remarks
Medium howitzer	Taisho 4 (1915) and later models	150mm (5.90in)	22	1,350	HE, AP, CW, Shrapnel, Smoke	80	7,560	65°	5°	6°	6,100	Box	
Medium howitzer	96 (1936)	150mm (5.90in)	22	—	HE, AP, Shrapnel, Smoke	80	11,400	75°	7°	30°	8,765	Split	
Medium gun	14 (1925)	105mm (4.14in)	—	2,040	HE, AP, Shrapnel, Chemical	33	14,500	43°	5°	30°	6,850	Split	Obsolescent in 1938 Tractor drawn
Medium gun	92 (1932)	105mm (4.14in)	—	2,500	HE, AP, Chemical (HE) Smoke	33	20,100	48°	10°	30°	6,600	Split	Tractor drawn
Gun	89 (1929)	150mm (5.90in)	—	—	HE, AP, Shrapnel	80	22,000	—	—	47°	16,500	Split	Tractor drawn
Howitzer	45 (1912)	240mm (9.44in)	—	—	HE	400	11,000	—	—	—	—	—	Transported in 10 vehicles
Rly gun	—	240mm (9.44in)	—	3,560	HE	440	54,500	—	—	—	35 tons	—	Several types reported
Howitzer	—	30cm (11.8in)	196in	1,310	HE	880	12,750	46°	—	—	14.7 tons	—	
Howitzer	—	30cm (11.8in)	324in	1,140	HE	1,100	16,600	48°	—	—	19.7 tons	—	
Siege howitzer	—	41cm (16in)	538in	1,760	HE	2,200	21,200	45°	—	—	80 tons	—	

Japanese Mortars

Model	Calibre	Length	Total Weight (lb)	Range (yd)	Ammunition	Remarks
98 (1938)*	50mm (1.97in)	2ft 1in	48	450 approx (Stick bomb) 320 approx (Demolition tube)	(a) HE stick 14lb (b) Demolition tube 18.5 lb	Smooth bore Range slide att to muzzle
Taisho 11	70mm (2.75in)	2ft 6in	133.75	1,700 max	HE 4.7lb Propellant in base Operation similar to Model 98 HE shell	Rifled barrel Obsolescent in 1940
Barrage	70mm (2.75in)	4ft (approx)	25 (approx)	4,000ft vertical	Projectile contains 7 bombs each with a parachute	Smooth bore Chiefly for use against low-flying aircraft
97 (1937)*	81mm (3.18in)	4ft 1.5in	145	3,100 max (1) 550 (approx) min (1) 1,300 max (2) 210 min (2)	6.93lb (1) 14lb (2) (1) Light shell (2) Heavy shell	Smooth bore Interchangeable with US M43 81mm ammunition
99 (1939)* small	81mm (3.18in)	2ft 1.25in (barrel)	52	2,000 max	HE smoke 6.93lb	Smooth bore Trigger firing mechanism Can fire US M43 81mm bombs with range of 2,500yd
94 (1934)*	90mm (3.54in)	4ft 4in (barrel)	342	4,150 max 600 min (approx)	HE Incendiary 11.5lb	Smooth bore U-shaped recoil system Obsolescent in 1940
97 (1937)* light	90mm (3.54in)	4ft 3.37in (barrel)	233	4,150 max	HE 11.5lb Incendiary	Replaced by Model 94
93 (1933)	150mm (5.9in)	4ft 11in (barrel)	220(barrel) Total 558	Sighted to 2,100m (2,296yd)	56lb	Smooth bore
97 (1937)	150mm (5.9in)	4ft 11in (barrel)	Total 778	Sighted to 2,100m (2,296yd)	HE	Smooth bore
98 (1938)	250mm (9.8in)	2ft 10in (spigot)	900	1,000 max (estimated)	Model 98 HE shell 674lb, 320mm (12.5in) diam	Spigot mortar

* These are the infantry mortars described on pages 53-59

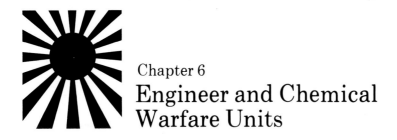

Chapter 6
Engineer and Chemical Warfare Units

Engineers

As the field companies of the non-specialised Japanese divisional engineers were frequently overworked, any extensive engineering duties normally had to be carried out by independent engineer regiments. Such regiments, *Dokuritsu Kohei Rentai*, included units for general engineering employment as well as specialists.

In 1940 the Imperial Army had several types of multi-purpose independent engineer regiments — each carrying out different engineering tasks such as bridge-building, operating landing barges etc. However, as the war progressed the system changed and a distinct series of different units were raised and trained in the more specialised types of work. Consequently by 1944 three different types of independent engineer regiments existed. First of all there were those regiments, battalions and companies, which were designed for employment on general field engineer tasks — although some of the regiments and battalions might well include specialist companies in their organisation. Similarly equipped to the divisional field engineer regiments, such regiments in an advance would take over the tasks and responsibilities of the divisional engineers' regiments as the division moved on. They were expected to tackle any military engineering job, to make the most of the light miscellaneous equipment they carried and to improvise with local materials. Every engineer carried a rifle and was trained to fight as an infantryman. Such 'general purpose' units also carried a number of machine guns for local and anti-aircraft protection and pack flame-throwers were often carried on a scale of one per platoon.

The second type of independent engineer unit — battalions (*Dokuritsu Kohei Daitai*, and companys (*Dokuritsu Kohei Chutai*) — had a specialised role. Engineer battalions, equipped with barges or landing craft, consisting of two companies and a stores platoon, functioned as shipping and sea transport units. Other companies specialised in surmounting river obstacles, and these bridge-building and river-crossing units were usually sent up to assist the divisional engineers when their services were called for. Their job was to carry heavy bridge and boat equipment and they were organised on both horse or motor transport establishments.

Left: Folding boat M95. /*IWM*

Below: Medium tank M2595 being ferried across a river in China. /*IWM*

Bottom: Small pontoon bridge. /*IWM*

Top right: Amphibious tank. /*IWM*

Bottom right: Amphibious truck. /*IWM*

Another of the specialised engineer units was the shipping engineer regiment, the *Sempaku Kohei Rentai*, which was responsible for operating barges for the Japanese Army. Army shipping groups, which were branches of the army shipping administration, controlled the administration and movement of the shipping engineer regiments as a whole. Since, however, the shipping engineers were an integral part both of landing operations and of water-borne supply, they frequently came under the operational control of the local field commander and a number of them, renamed 'sea transport units', eventually became permanently attached to certain divisions.

The shipping engineer regiment consisted of a headquarters, three companies, and a service company. The three companies were each organised into a headquarters and four platoons; the platoon contained four to seven boat sections and a service section. Each boat section operated a landing craft or barge, usually one of the three main types of landing craft shown in the following table. The Daihatsu Army Type 'A' — a vessel of clumsy appearance but proven usefulness and versatility — was probably the most widely used type. In addition, the various headquarters probably had a number of armoured boats (armed with a 57mm (2.24in) gun), reserve landing craft, and various small craft bringing the regimental total to 120-150 vessels.

Types of Japanese Landing Craft

Type	Crew	Armament	Employment
Tokubetsu Daihatsu Special large craft	8-10	20mm (.787in) Machine cannon, 4 LMGs	Often used to carry tanks, heavy guns and other heavy material
Daihatsu Army Type 'A' large craft	5-7	One or more HMG or 20mm (.787in) or 37mm (1.45in) gun	Transport of troops and supplies
Shohatsu Types 'B' and 'C' small craft	3-5	MMG	Principally for landing troops in face of enemy, or landing light stores

Summarising their role: Japanese shipping engineers were responsible for moving troops in water-borne operations, supply by water, and the unloading of ships at anchorages. In the island war in the SW Pacific, therefore, they were extremely important.

Also numbered among the specialist engineer units was a variety of field and road construction units, the *Yasen Kenchikutai* and *Yasen Dorotai*, stevedore and 'anchorage' units at ports, field well drilling companies etc. In fact most of these units consisted of a few trained and armed Japanese engineers in charge of coolie labour.

Finally, the remaining type of engineers was specially designed and equipped for assault engineering with armoured vehicles. With an

Japanese Engineer Equipment Principal Demolition Equipment and Mines

Equipment	Model	Dimensions	Total weight	Explosive	Remarks
100gm demolition charge	—	2in by 2in by 1in	100gm (3.5oz)	Cast picric acid	Wrapped in waxed paper
1kg demolition charge	—	2.875in by 2.125in by 8in	1,300gm (2lb 12oz)	2lb 3oz	Charge contained in zinc case
Magnetic Atk demolition charge	99 (1939)	Diam 4.75in Thickness 1.5in	2lb 11oz	1.5lb TNT in eight blocks	Also an infantry weapon, known as 'magnetic Atk bomb' for attachment to a metal surface
Mine, anti-personnel Atk	93 (1933)	Diam 6.75in	3lb	2lb	Igniter provided with shear wires of various strengths from 20lb or less to 250lb
Mine, anti-personnel Atk	Dutch (PW2-41)	Diam 8.25in Thickness 3.5in	9.5lb	5.5lb TNT	Firing load about 50lb
Mine, Atk Yardstick	—	Length 36in Width 3.5in	10.5lb	6lb picric acid	Elliptical cross-section Three or four igniters Firing pressure (estimated) 336lb on any one igniter
Bangalore torpedo	99 (1939)	Length oa (one tube) 46in	(one tube) 10lb	TNT and RDX	Several tubes could be attached end to end. Pull type delay double-igniter
Mine, land, non-metallic	3 (1943)	(a) Diam 10.5in Height 3.5in (b) Diam 8.5in Height 3.5in	(a)? 10.5lb	Amatol 50/50 or ammonium nitrate HE (a) larger type 6.5lb (b) smaller type 4.5lb	Body made of terra-cotta Igniter made of plastic, combined push and pull type
Mine, anti-boat hemispherical	98 (1938)	Diam (base) 20in Height 10.5in	106.5lb	46lb trinitroanisol (TNA)	Two lead alloy horns
Mine, anti-boat 'Tea-Kettle'	2 (1942)	Diam (base) 14.25in (top) 7in Height oa 16in	65-70lb	22lb TNA/dipicrylamine 60/40	Black painted Single lead alloy horn (chemical-electrical) igniter Actuating pressure 150lb approx

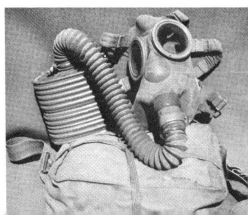

Above: Landing craft. Note the aero-engine propulsion. A tankette can be seen on one of the craft in the middle distance. / *IWM*

Left: Navy type gas mask.

Below left: Civil Defence corps gas mask.

Below: Army type gas mask.

Right: Army service respirator. / *IWM*

establishment of about 1,000 all ranks, this regiment was organised into three companies each with 175 men and four tankettes as well as 14 lorries to carry specialised demolition equipment, including explosives, flame-throwers etc; and a regimental ammunition train with a reserve of three tankettes and 17 lorries for the carriage of stores.

Chemical Warfare Units

Although the Japanese did not use gas in World War II, they were certainly capable of doing so. Moreover, they were also able to defend themselve, if the Allies had engaged in chemical warfare. On the one hand they had established factories for poison gas manufacture and created a number of specialised chemical warfare units which could have formed the basis of an offensive chemical warfare organisation. On the other hand, before hostilities started they had developed anti-gas measures and issued an efficient respirator to their services.

Each Japanese division had a number of trained 'gas personnel' who were responsible for the defensive aspects and the offensive units consisted of a 'gas battalion' and a number of independent gas companies. The men of these gas units were armed and equipped as medium and heavy mortar units, and if the Japanese had decided to use gas it would undoubtedly have been projected by means of these weapons.

At the beginning of the war a few divisions also had decontamination units with equipment (in vehicles and trailers) for dealing with con-taminated clothing and for decontaminating roads. As the war progressed, however, and no gas warfare developed these units tended to disappear and their personnel was absorbed as infantry reinforcements.

Above: Tankette Type 97 converted to armoured personnel carrier. / *IWM*

Centre right: 6-ton tractor Model 98 used to pull heavy artillery. / *IWM*

Bottom right: Half-track vehicle, probably not of Japanese manufacture and not in general service. / *IWM*

Chapter 7
Special Forces

Cavalry

Japanese cavalry deserves a brief mention if only because the Imperial Army maintained a number of independent cavalry brigades right up to the end of the war. These brigades were formations of two regiments and supporting arms. The horsed regiments consisted of four sabre companiess and one machine gun company, sabre companies each having a nominal strength of 186 while the machine gun company had an establishment of 167 all ranks to man its four medium machine gun and one anti-tank platoons. Sabre companies, organised into a company headquarters and three platoons, had eight light machine guns and four 'knee-mortars' in addition to the carbines carried by individual troopers.

To support the two cavalry regiments the independent cavalry brigades had a horse artillery regiment equipped with eight 75mm mountain or field guns, a light tank unit of 12 light tanks, an anti-tank company, and sometimes a machine cannon company with four anti-aircraft machine guns.

Only a few of these brigades existed and all but one of them was stationed in Manchuria.

Paratroops and Airborne Forces

Both the Japanese Army and the Imperial Navy had paratroops, the basic army parachute unit being the regiment (*Teishin Rentai*, literally 'Raiding Regiment') — commanded by a major or lieutenant-colonel, with a jumping strength of about 600, and organised into a headquarters, three companies and a supply section.

The combat uniform of army parachutists was a dark khaki overall, web equipment, crash helmet, and strong rubber or leather boots. The parachute regiment, when employed against the Allies in the opening stages of the Japanese war (at Palembang and Koepang, February 1942), was armed with pistol, hand grenades, rifle and bayonet (the rifleman carrying 30 to 40 rounds on the jump), light machine gun and 2in knee-mortar. A light pack flame-thrower was added later.

Japanese doctrine on the use of airborne troops did not differ from that of Western armies, and an embryo airborne formation known as the 'Airborne Group' (*Teishin Dan* — literally 'Raiding Group') was formed during the war. This formation comprised two parachute regiments, two squadrons of aircraft to carry the parachutists, and a glider regiment.

Amphibious Brigades*

In 1943, a number of 'amphibious brigades' were raised to meet the special problems of defending outlying groups of islands in the Japanese Empire and those under Japanese occupation. Such formations, commanded by a major-general, had an infantry component of three heavily armed independent infantry battalions (all drawn from independent garrison units) and supporting units of tanks, dual-purpose machine cannon, engineers, and signals. It had no brigade artillery unit, but each infantry battalion had a gun company as well as a mortar company.

Its transport was its most remarkable feature. The amphibious brigade transport unit was identical with the 'sea transport unit' which appeared during the winter 1943-44 in a number of divisions which were specially organised for island warfare. In effect the amphibious brigade transport unit was originally a shipping engineer regiment, reorganised and expanded for its new duties. Equipped with barges or landing-craft, it was about 1,500 strong and consisted of four transport companies, an escort company, and a material depot or stores park.

The Japanese intention in forming these amphibious brigades was probably to use them as a mobile reserve, which could be held at some central point of a group of islands and rushed to any point threatened with Allied attack. But often from circumstances outside their control their intentions did not work out in practice, and the forces intended for counter-attack found themselves tied down to static defence. One amphibious brigade was intended for some such role in the Marshall Islands, but in fact had to be split up and used to garrison four atolls.

The men of these brigades were armed with the usual run of conventional weapons — rifles, machine guns, 81mm mortars, 75mm mountain guns, 37mm anti-tank guns. But the amphibious infantry battalions were stronger in heavy weapons than the battalions in standard infantry divisions.

Independent Motorised Brigades

A special and unique independent mixed brigade, with motor transport for all arms, was met and destroyed by Allied Forces in the SW Pacific in 1943. Its infantry component was an infantry regiment of three battalions, each of four companies. (The regiment had, until the formation of the brigade, formed part of an infantry division.) The supporting arms included medium artillery and an abnormally strong brigade tank unit of 15 medium and 50 light tanks.

---

* The term 'amphibious brigade' is used in this context for convenience, but is not a literal equivalent: *Kaijo Kido Ryodan*, the Japanese term, means literally 'Mobile seaborne brigade'.

1 Scout car 95 (1933).
2 Truck Model 81.
3 Truck Model 94A and 94B (1934).
4 Truck Model 2601.
(Scale 1mm = 1m) / *Bryan Fosten*

Below: Japanese water truck. / *IWM*

South Seas Detachment

A series of numbered defence forces (called *Nanpo Shitai* — literally meaning 'Southern Area Detached Unit') were created from existing regiments for duties on various island groups in the SW Pacific area.

Three of the South Sea detachments consisted of two infantry battalions and a small tank unit (strength 55; eight light tanks). Detachment HQ had a signals section and a transport section. The battalions had three weak rifle companies only 103 strong, a machine gun company and a battalion gun company. In one of these detachments the battalion machine gun companies were found to include two anti-tank platoons, while the battalion gun company consisted of two anti-tank platoons and two mortar platoons. In this instance, all the artillery and other supporting arms which were available locally had been added to the force.

Two other South Seas detachments had a bigger original establishment, though they were based on the same battalion of 531 all ranks with a rifle/LMG company of 103. They had three battalions instead of two and an engineer company. Finally, one South Seas detachment was organised with only one battalion, a tank company, and detachment headquarters.

Land Forces of the Japanese Navy

Many of the landing operations carried out by the Japanese in the course of their East Asia and Pacific conquests were performed by land forces of the Imperial Navy. Having seized innumerable Pacific islands the Navy then found itself committed to their defence, and consequently the forces originally created for seaborne attack had to be reorganised for garrison and defensive duties on groups of islands in the Pacific and the China Sea. They were, in fact, anti-landing forces, although they continued to be known as Special Naval Landing Forces.

The organisation and strength of such forces was variable, since the Japanese reorganised them for defensive missions as the need arose, and strengthened particular forces as the situation required it. Principal weapons of two such forces, the *Maizuru 2* and the *Yakosuka 7* Special Naval Landing Forces, engaged in the defence of New Georgia, were conventional army equipments — rifles, machine guns, mortars, anti-tank and anti-aircraft guns.

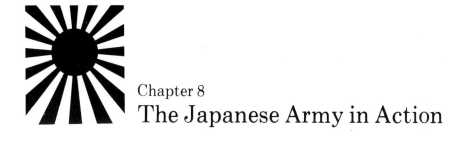

Chapter 8
The Japanese Army in Action

The conclusion to be derived from the previous chapters is that Japanese weapons in World War II were, on the whole, below Western standards in quality. But they existed in quantities sufficient for the needs of the Imperial Army, and the soldiers who employed them were tough and generally well-trained. It is not proposed to describe the tactics used by the Japanese; sufficient to say they were daring in attack, stubborn in defence and even when the position seemed hopeless they usually went on fighting to the death.

Our concern here is rather more with the way they employed their equipment, and its suitability. To begin with it must be appreciated that Japanese soldiers were not all either the skinny, scrawny, or chubby and bow-legged characters depicted in wartime propaganda cartoons. Some of them were magnificent examples of what a Spartan existence can do towards improving physique. Nearly all Japanese are athletic enthusiasts; indeed, Kung-Fu expertise apart, some of the finest acrobats and athletes come from Honshu. Apart from their athletic prowess, however, the Japanese soldiers of World War II were accustomed to long hours of hard work, and if they were properly directed a squad of Japanese infantrymen could dig their way through a mountain — as the bunkers and prodigious earthworks in Burma, Guadalcanal or Okinawa testified.

In effect the peasant background of the average Japanese soldier had other advantages. To men used to carrying 200lb of rice seedlings on their backs, lugging heavy equipment over long jungle trails was a very small problem. Battalion and regimental guns, and mountain artillery were manhandled into positions deep in the jungle and Allied troops often found themselves being shelled from unexpected directions. In appraising the staying power of his men for carrying operations of this nature the Japanese officer also deserves credit. The officers rarely underestimated the capabilities of their men, and Japanese infantry men were probably the first soldiers in the world to learn that there is no such thing as impenetrable jungle.

Columns of Japanese troops on the march never presented a very military appearance. The men tended to walk rather than to march, straggling to their destination in the quickest and least troublesome fashion. At halts they made themselves as comfortable as possible, and it was customary to

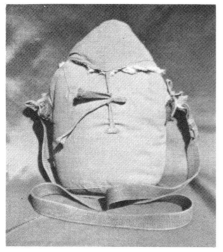

Above: Officer-type water-bottles.

Right: Troops' issue water-bottles.

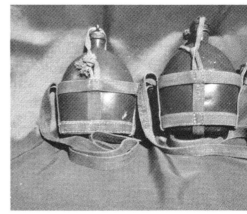

Below: Mess-tins.

pick items such as firewood up en route. Years of active service and realistic training instilled in the Japanese Imperial Army a healthy respect for results rather than appearances. As with the Israeli Army today, formal discipline was reserved for the parade ground; in the field emphasis was on marching and tactical training.

The Japanese knew how to live off the land, and to make the best of their environment. Apart from teams of 'comfort girls', the men in the field had few amenities. There were no mobile cinemas, no NAAFI, no PX; and the Japanese supply services did not send out large quantities of foodstuffs from metropolitan Japan. Expeditionary forces in Burma and China got their food by commandeering local supplies. In more remote areas the Japanese supplemented their rations by shooting and fishing; fish was often procured by the simple expedient of tossing a grenade into a jungle stream. Once they killed the game or fish they cut it up and cooked it either in their mess tins or in a piece of bamboo. Rice was usually cooked in the morning and Japanese soldiers always fed individually or in small tactical groups. There were no field kitchens in the Imperial Army, and no men were designated as cooks for fighting units. Every man in a field formation was a fighting soldier; there were no non-combatants or non-effective personnel. Every man was responsible for the preparation of his own food. Rice was a compact easily-carried ration. Usually it was carried in a sort of stocking, open at one end for pouring.

Japanese mess-tins generally had one or two trays which fitted under the lid; these and the lid served as 'plates'. Japanese water bottles were somewhat bigger than the British and American equivalent. And as they were hung on a separate sling and not attached to the rest of the man's personal equipment, the individual soldier could take a drink without undoing his belt while on the line of march. March discipline did not preclude him from doing so.

Every other item of the Japanese combat soldier's personal equipment — including his pack and horse-shoe blanket roll — was practical and adequate, though its appearance was not prepossessing. In Burma and Indo-China the infantry added much to their mobility by utilising every bit of civilian transport they could lay their hands on. Tarmac roads in these countries made bicycles especially useful. However, in places where no roads existed the Japanese continued to place a high value on such 'transport'. As most of them had never owned a cycle before, they were keen to keep the ones they had 'liberated'. In consequence, bicycles with Singapore registrations were found in remote jungle areas on Guadalcanal.

Just as their troops were reluctant to discard loot they had collected in the course of a campaign, so too were Japanese officers loath to be without their swords. Wherever they went these symbols of authority and status accompanied them. Pilots carried swords in their aircraft, visiting staff officers were never photographed without them, and all combatant officers of company commander and below wore them continuously. Some non-commissioned officers also carried swords, and every Japanese who did so also carried a silk cloth and cleaning material with which to polish the blade — many of which were hundreds of years old and treasured accordingly.

The Chinese used to speak disparagingly of the Japanese as 'Monkey People'. Whether or not the features of some Japanese justified the description, there was little doubt that many Japanese soldiers could swarm up trees with the ease of monkeys. Split-toed sandals made the climb easier — the tread on the soles enabling the man wearing them to retain a firm grip and the separated big toe feature allowing him to feel his footing much better than with boots or shoes. All accounts of battles in South-East Asia and the Pacific invariably refer to the effectiveness of Japanese snipers posted in trees. In fact the Japanese used trees more for observation purposes than for sniping, but when they did take up sniping positions in the trees they were often extremely difficult to locate and to dislodge. Not only were they camouflage-conscious, they would also tie themselves into positions, so that they remained in place even if wounded.

Fortunately for Allied troops the average Japanese infantryman was not a good shot and, for the technical reasons that have been described, his Arisaka rifle was not a good weapon for accurate shooting. But it was adequate, and the Japanese infantry developed an effective method of shooting from a squatting position which most British and American soldiers — less flexible in muscle and tendon than the Japanese — would have found awkward. This squatting position was never taught formally but presumably evolved in the field, as a natural adaptation of the Japanese civilian 'squat'. (Peasants squat down to talk to each other in rural Japan, and rest in the same position.)

In this respect the Japanese were always quick to try to adapt any method old or new. For example, when they found that barbed wire prevented them creeping up to Allied positions, and they were unable to cut their way through the wire without revealing their presence they adopted suicide tactics. Men detailed as wire-cutters would carry an explosive pack tied to their bodies. If they were shot, there was every possibility of the detonators on the explosive pack being hit at the same time. And if the individual was only wounded, as like or not he would pull out a safety pin and do the same thing — blowing away the wire he would not have time to cut. Many Japanese engineers who crawled up to Allied positions had suicide chaarges tied to their bodies with this idea in mind. Similarly when British tanks were deployed in Central Burma in 1944, and the Japanese realised that their anti-tank weapons could not cope with the threat, Japanese infantrymen were positioned across lines of approach as living anti-tank devices.*

But the Japanese will be remembered primarily for their offensive rather than defensive tactics in World War II. Japanese infantry won the war in China, Indo-China, Malaya and the Dutch East Indies and the Pacific — and subsequently lost it — with attacks which culminated in *Banzai*

---

* In the writer's experience these men were given an aircraft bomb and large stone with which to strike the nose fuse when a tank overran their position.

Left: Japanese soldier's haversack.

Below: Folding handcart for use by infantry. / *IWM*

charges. These assaults which proved so effective against the poorly-armed Chinese and inexperienced Allied troops were the outstanding feature of Japanese tactics. Based on the 19th century concept that cold steel could match fire power it became the very symbol of Japanese stupidity. For these tactics Japanese infantry weapons and the training associated with them were more than adequate. But a determined enemy can always stop a *Banzai* charge and mow down his opponents even with a bolt-action rifle. With a self-loading or automatic weapon a *Banzai* charge could be converted into a massacre.

When the Japanese realised this and were compelled to revert to the defensive they and their outmoded weapons were at a disadvantage. As always their soldiers were brave, extremely stubborn, and well disciplined. Moreover they could still fight and dig well.

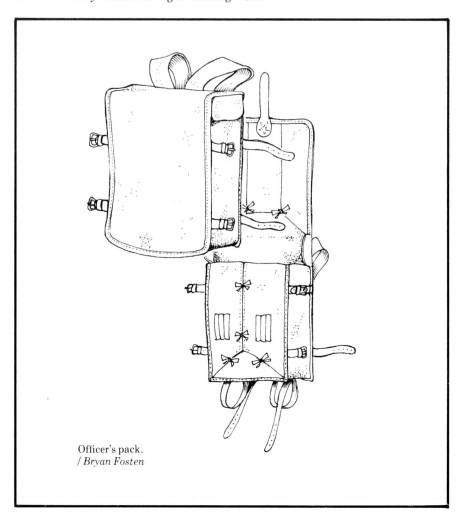

Officer's pack.
/ *Bryan Fosten*

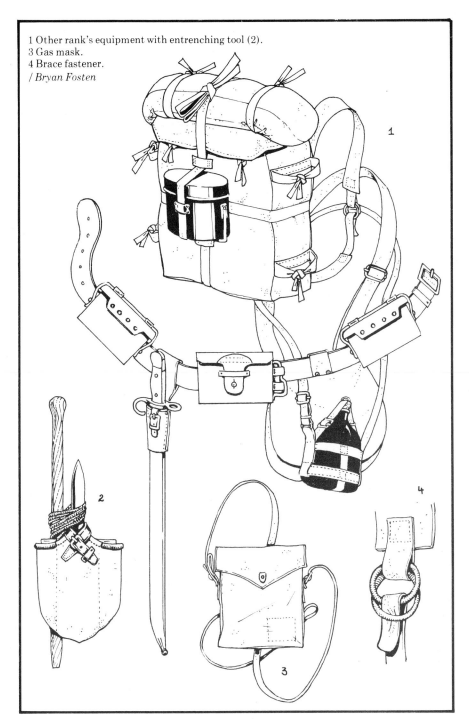

1 Other rank's equipment with entrenching tool (2).
3 Gas mask.
4 Brace fastener.
/ *Bryan Fosten*

Right: 70mm M92 Battalion gun in action. / *IWM*

Below: A Type 92 7.7mm medium machine gun in action. Notice that even in these circumstances the officer retains his sword. / *IWM*

Appendix 1

Organisation of Japanese Infantry Divisions

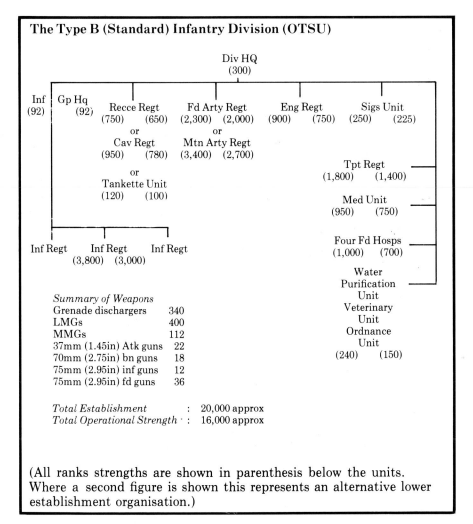

The Type B (Standard) Infantry Division (OTSU)

Div HQ
(300)

Inf (92)	Gp Hq (92)	Recce Regt (750) (650)	Fd Arty Regt (2,300) (2,000)	Eng Regt (900) (750)	Sigs Unit (250) (225)

or
Cav Regt
(950) (780)

or
Mtn Arty Regt
(3,400) (2,700)

or
Tankette Unit
(120) (100)

Tpt Regt
(1,800) (1,400)

Med Unit
(950) (750)

Inf Regt   Inf Regt   Inf Regt
(3,800) (3,000)

Four Fd Hosps
(1,000) (700)

Water
Purification
Unit
Veterinary
Unit
Ordnance
Unit
(240) (150)

Summary of Weapons
Grenade dischargers   340
LMGs   400
MMGs   112
37mm (1.45in) Atk guns 22
70mm (2.75in) bn guns   18
75mm (2.95in) inf guns 12
75mm (2.95in) fd guns   36

Total Establishment   :   20,000 approx
Total Operational Strength :   16,000 approx

(All ranks strengths are shown in parenthesis below the units.
Where a second figure is shown this represents an alternative lower
establishment organisation.)

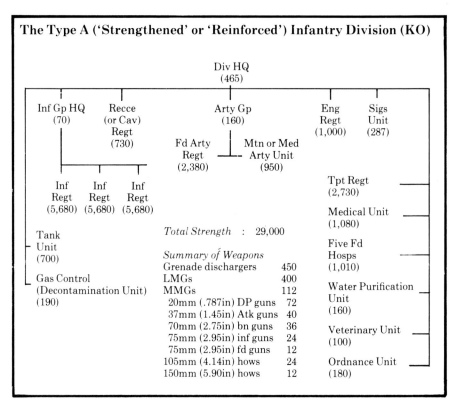

The Type A ('Strengthened' or 'Reinforced') Infantry Division (KO)

Div HQ
(465)

Inf Gp HQ (70)

Recce (or Cav) Regt (730)

Inf Regt (5,680) Inf Regt (5,680) Inf Regt (5,680)

Tank Unit (700)

Gas Control (Decontamination Unit) (190)

Arty Gp (160)

Fd Arty Regt (2,380) Mtn or Med Arty Unit (950)

Total Strength : 29,000

Summary of Weapons

Grenade dischargers	450
LMGs	400
MMGs	112
20mm (.787in) DP guns	72
37mm (1.45in) Atk guns	40
70mm (2.75in) bn guns	36
75mm (2.95in) inf guns	24
75mm (2.95in) fd guns	12
105mm (4.14in) hows	24
150mm (5.90in) hows	12

Eng Regt (1,000)   Sigs Unit (287)

Tpt Regt (2,730)

Medical Unit (1,080)

Five Fd Hosps (1,010)

Water Purification Unit (160)

Veterinary Unit (100)

Ordnance Unit (180)

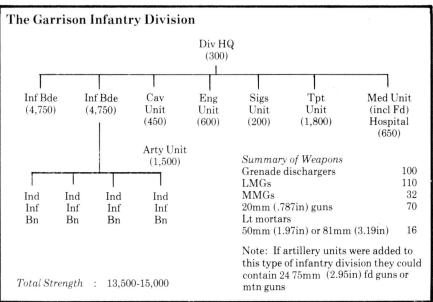

The Garrison Infantry Division

Div HQ
(300)

Inf Bde (4,750)   Inf Bde (4,750)   Cav Unit (450)   Eng Unit (600)   Sigs Unit (200)   Tpt Unit (1,800)   Med Unit (incl Fd) Hospital (650)

Arty Unit (1,500)

Ind Inf Bn   Ind Inf Bn   Ind Inf Bn   Ind Inf Bn

Summary of Weapons

Grenade dischargers	100
LMGs	110
MMGs	32
20mm (.787in) guns	70
Lt mortars	
50mm (1.97in) or 81mm (3.19in)	16

Note: If artillery units were added to this type of infantry division they could contain 24 75mm (2.95in) fd guns or mtn guns

Total Strength : 13,500-15,000

Appendix 2

Organisation of Japanese Independent Formations

Organisation of a typical Japanese Independent Brigade
(All ranks strength is shown in parenthesis)

Comd- Maj-Gen
HQ- C of S Colonel
(203) Adjt Major

| Inf Bn (931) | Inf Bn (931) | Inf Bn (931) | | Inf Bn (931) | Inf Bn (931) | Arty Unit (360) | Engr Unit (180) | Sigs Unit (178) |

Bn HQ (93)

HQ (70)

| 1 Coy (176) | 2 Coy (176) | 3 Coy (176) | 4 Coy (176) |

Heavy Weapons Unit (134)

1 Coy (145)
Gun or Mortar Coy
8 mortars
or 4 Mountain
guns

2 Coy (145)
Usually Mortar Coy
8 mortars

Establishment : 5,580 all ranks

Estimate of principal weapons

	Inf Bn	Arty Unit	Bde Total (Bde of five bns)
LMGs	36	—	180
50mm (1.97in) grenade dischargers	36	—	180
MMGs	4	—	16
20mm (.787in) machine cannon	4	—	16
75mm (2.95in) guns or 105mm (4.14in) hows	—	See (2) below	
Mortars	—	See (2) and (3) below	

(1) The number of infantry battalions varied between four and six. Brigade strength varied between 4,400 and 6,500 according to composition.

(2) The brigade artillery unit in brigades of this type could be a gun or howitzer unit or a mortar unit. Alternatives were:

(a) Two companies of 75mm (2.95in) mtn guns or 105mm (4.14in) hows (total eight guns or hows)

or

(b) One company of four mtn guns and one company of mortars. The mortar company had either four 150mm (5.9in) medium mortars or eight lighter mortars 81mm (3.18in) or 90mm (3.54in)

or

(c) Two companies of mortars (total eight or sixteen mortars according to calibre)

or

(d) One company only, armed with four medium mortars or eight 81mm or 90mm mortars.

(3) Mortars were included also in the infantry battalions, either in the heavy weapons unit or in a mortar platoon of the infantry companies.

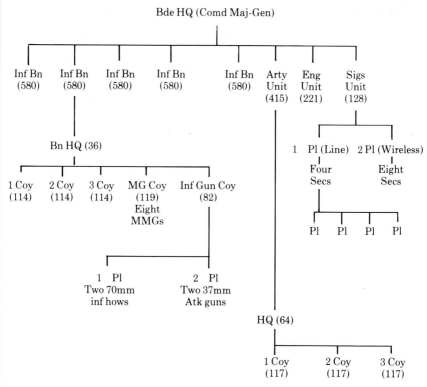

Organisation of a Japanese Independent Mixed Regiment
(All ranks strength is shown in parenthesis below each unit)

Bde HQ (Comd Maj-Gen)

| Inf Bn (580) | Inf Bn (580) | Inf Bn (580) | Inf Bn (580) | Inf Bn (580) | Arty Unit (415) | Eng Unit (221) | Sigs Unit (128) |

Bn HQ (36)

1 Coy (114)   2 Coy (114)   3 Coy (114)   MG Coy (119) Eight MMGs   Inf Gun Coy (82)

1 Pl Two 70mm inf hows   2 Pl Two 37mm Atk guns

1 Pl (Line) Four Secs   2 Pl (Wireless) Eight Secs

Pl   Pl   Pl   Pl

HQ (64)

1 Coy (117)   2 Coy (117)   3 Coy (117)

Each Arty Coy had four 75mm field or mountain guns or 105mm howitzers.

The total of all ranks in this example was : 3,800

Summary of weapons

	Inf Bn	Arty Unit	Total (five bns)
LMGS	12		60
50mm (1.97in) grenade dischargers	16		80
MMGs (type 92, with AA mount)	8		40
37mm (1.45in) Atk guns	2		10
70mm (2.75in) infantry hows (battalion guns)	2		10
75mm (2.95in) fd or mtn guns or 105mm (4.14in) hows		12	12

Possible additions were a tank unit (92 all ranks), an anti-aircraft company (170 all rank) and extra artillery or anti-aircraft artillery.

Appendix 3

Organisation of a Japanese Tank Regiment

Japanese tank regiments operated in Malaya and one was identified in New Britain in 1943, but most of them were stationed in Manchuria.

The organisation was not necessarily uniform and varied according to the types of tanks with which it was equipped. Usually, however, it consisted of three companies.

The commander of the regiment was a colonel or a lieutenant-colonel; and the company commanders were either captains or lieutenants.

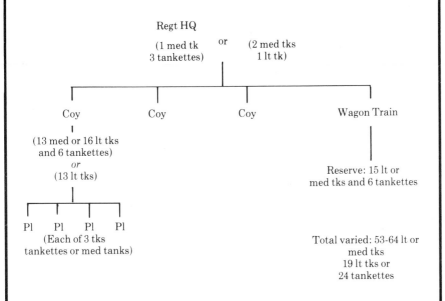

Total personnel strength : 850 approx

General

By the end of the war the Japanese had come to regard the medium tank as the basis of their armoured organisations, the tank company as the battle unit, and the tank regiment as the tactical unit.

Appendix 4
Japanese Military Terms and Characters

---

important Military Characters

Infantry	步兵 *Hohei*	Cavalry	騎兵 *Kihei*	Artillery	砲兵 *Hohei*
Division	師團 *Shidan*	Brigade	旅團 *Ryodan*	Regiment	聯隊 *Rentai*
Battalion	大隊 *Daitai*	Company	中隊 *Chutai*	Platoon	小隊 *Shotai*

Characters used in the nomenclature of Army stores

Date

		Numbers			
年號 =	Nengo	〇 = 0		七 =	7
明治 =	Meiji	一 = 1		八 =	8
大正 =	Taisho	二 = 2		九 =	9
昭和 =	Shōwa	三 = 3		十 =	10
神武紀 =	Anniversary of Jimmu	四 = 4		十一 =	11
		五 = 5		十二 =	12
年 =	Year	六 = 6			
年内 =	Within the Year	廿 or 二〇 = 20			
		一廿 or 二一 = 21			
月 =	Month	二廿 or 二二 = 22			
日 =	Day	卅 or 三〇 = 30			
		一卅 or 三一 = 31			
式 =	Pattern	二卅 or 三二 = 32			